SO

A fe

Amy Vaughan-Spencer

Cover photos by Craig Aitchison
Illustrations by Ellypop Illustration

Printed by Catford Print Centre, London

Soulcat.co.uk

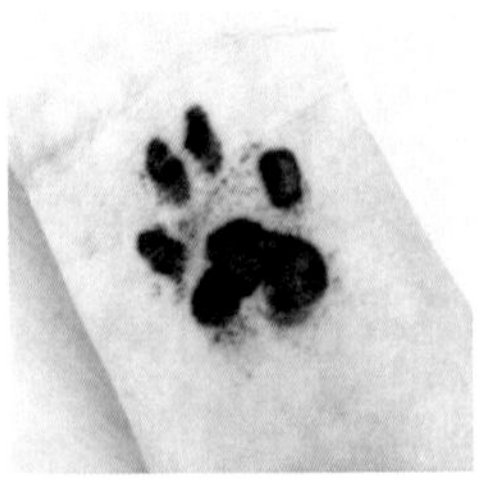

Soulcat Publishing

Printed in the United Kingdom

A CIP catalogue record for this book is available from the British Library

ISBN 13: 978-1-7398016-1-8

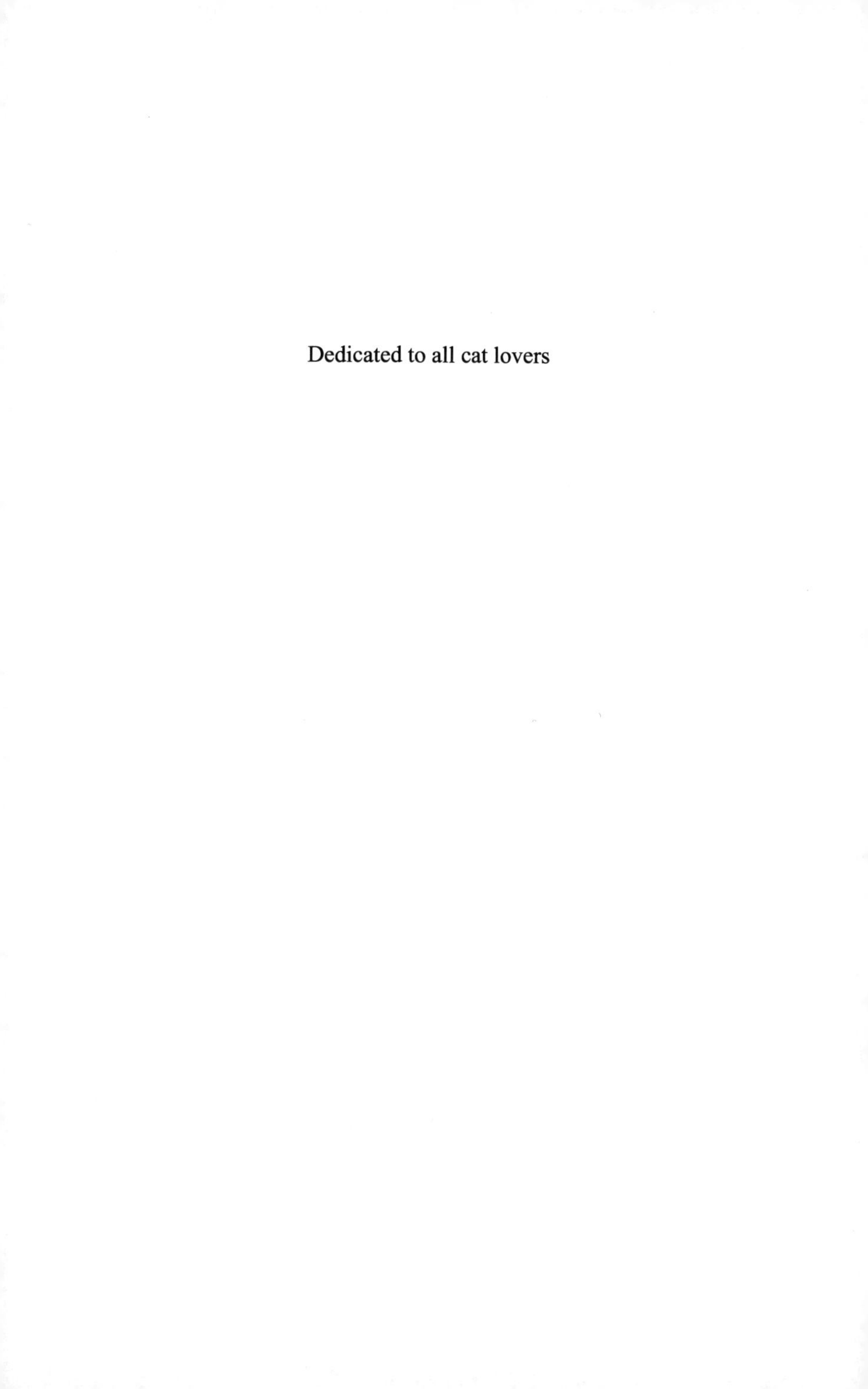

Dedicated to all cat lovers

PART 1

FOREWORD

'One day I was counting the cats and I absent-mindedly counted myself.'

— Bobbie Ann Mason, Shiloh and Other Stories

On July 21st, 2013, my beloved cat Molly passed away. She had been my affectionate and loyal companion for nine happy years, and I was completely unprepared for her sudden death. In need of an outlet for my grief, I sat down to write her a letter. I planned on composing a note to keep forever, to read in years to come, worried my memories and emotions would fade like an old photograph on the mantel, its vibrant colours bleached out by the sun.

The more I wrote, the more anecdotes surfaced of sweet moments and funny stories. My letter developed into a document of our life together, which was more eventful than that of most cats and their humans.

Once written, it seemed a shame not to share Molly's story, and friends encouraged me to publish it. I've changed the names of those I've been unable to request permission from, but everything else is fact. It's a 'tail' of a unique friendship, filled with adventures. Find a comfy chair, grab a hot drink, and prepare to fall in love with the sweetest cat I've ever known.

My dearest darling Molly,

You slipped away from me so suddenly I didn't have the chance to say goodbye. I hope you could hear my voice and feel me stroking your head as you left this world, and I hope you are now in a happier place, free from the confines of a faulty but perfectly beautiful body. For nine years you were the one constant in my life. Every day you greeted me with your raspy meow and your saucer-like eyes, waking me up for breakfast in the morning and snuggling goodnight before we went to sleep. Every day I miss you.

CHAPTER ONE:

Glasgow, 2004

'You had me at Meow.'

— Fluffy Desire

You came into my life for a long weekend while your owners went away on holiday. It was a balmy August in Glasgow, where I lived with my boyfriend, Craig, in the West End of the city. The West End is 'the posh bit', with quirky independent shops, popular bars and restaurants, and long residential streets lined with terraces of beautiful big sandstone houses. Technically, we were more Northwest than West of the centre, but I liked to pretend we resided in the fancy part. Our flat was on Sandbank Crescent, a secluded cul-de-sac sandwiched between council estates, tucked behind the busy Maryhill Road, with a canal silently sweeping past on one side.

I was twenty-five and on a break from my career as a theatrical stage manager, which had taken me around the UK with various plays and operas. Craig and I had met while I was rehearsing for a tour in Scotland, and afterwards we dated long-distance. He lived with his family just outside Glasgow and I was based partly in my hometown of Guildford, in Surrey, and partly in London, while also travelling the country with shows. When it came to moving in together, we planned on settling in London, but he had a good job in a local production studio and didn't want to leave it. Since my work was contract-based and transient, it made more sense for me to move north.

I loved Glasgow for its eclectic architecture, cultural vibe and welcoming atmosphere. The locals are often considered tough and antagonistic, due to their impassioned competitiveness over football, linked with sectarianism, and their aggressive-sounding accent, which leads people to assume the worst. Having spent a lot of time in London, where making eye contact with a stranger is a mortal sin, I found it unnerving when strangers in my new city chatted to me at bus stops and in the streets. Naturally suspicious if someone looked at me and smiled, I was pleasantly surprised to discover they were just really friendly. Glaswegians belie their reputation by being some of the most affable folk you can meet.

Soon after relocating, I found some work at the Royal Concert Hall, before taking on a three-month contract with Scottish Opera On Tour. Then I found myself at a loose end. Having trained 'down south', and with no contacts in the regional rep circuit, I struggled to get my foot in the proverbial stage-door.

I took a part-time job as a medical receptionist in a doctor's surgery, alongside creating a website for fellow touring theatre staff. The clinic occupied a beautiful grand building on a leafy avenue in the West End (the actual posh bit). While one receptionist stood at the small front desk booking in patients, four others worked in the office behind, answering calls and filing paperwork. I soon learned why medical receptionists are renowned for being miserable and short-tempered, as the phones rang off the hook all day with patients making impossible demands and failing to understand why prescription requests couldn't be processed instantly. My colleagues, however, were all lovely, and we kept each other sane with idle gossip and conversations revolving around what we'd be having for dinner that evening.

One afternoon, as I was sorting patient notes into their corresponding files, I overheard the office manager, Jeanette, discussing her upcoming family break.

'Molly will have to come along wi' us,' she said.

'Um, sorry,' I interrupted, 'you're going to take your cat camping?' I didn't understand how that would work.

'We'll have nae choice, there'll be nobody at home, and we can't afford a cattery.'

'I'll look after her if you like.' I said. 'She can stay with us.'

'Are you sure?'

'Of course! I'd love to have her for a few days. We had cats in the house all through my childhood, I miss having them around.'

'Well, don't make a rash decision, I wouldnae want to put you out. Talk it over with Craig and let me know.'

Jeanette assumed it would be a burden for us to cat-sit, but we relished the opportunity to have a bundle of fur in the flat for a few days. Craig's family had two feline members, and he missed them, despite having moved only a few miles away. We agreed that having a pet makes a house feel like more of a home.

Jeanette and I conducted your handover outside the surgery, from her car to mine, on my morning off. She gave me your bed, litter tray, some food and a couple of toys, before lifting out your cat carrier. In the shadows at the back of the box, I caught flashes of white and brown fur as you cowered in the far corner. I drove you home as carefully as if I had a newborn baby on the rear seat.

Our rented flat was about ten years old, purpose-built and decorated in standard magnolia with sea green carpets. I would have loved to have lived in a traditional tenement building, but Craig and I had a limited budget, and we had found nothing else we could afford larger than a shoe box. Sandbank Crescent was three miles outside the city centre and half that from the prestigious West End; far enough out to get twice the square feet for our money, but close enough for a short bus ride in either direction.

The flat was in the middle of a three-storey block. Our front door opened onto a long hallway, with the main bedroom and the living room off to the right, the spare bedroom and bathroom to the left, and a sizeable kitchen at the far end. Being modern, it lacked character, but we made it our own with a random assortment of accumulated furniture. One of Craig's relatives had given us a large cream sofa and matching armchair. My mum gave me a moving-in gift of a rattan Papasan chair with a big comfy red cushion. We had a pine TV unit, coffee and side tables, and some Ikea bookshelves to complete the space. Craig was a keen and talented photographer, so along with some artwork I already had, the walls displayed some of his original landscapes.

On the living room floor, we opened your carrier, stood back and waited, giving you space to emerge. After several pensive minutes, you gathered enough confidence and curiosity to step out. Craig and I had peeked through the metal grill door and spotted that your small white face was crowned with tabby patches above a pair of large green eyes. Tentatively sniffing your strange new surroundings, you entered the room, paw by paw, revealing a beautiful petite, slender frame. More dark splashes of tabby adorned your snowy back and covered your tail. You were scared and nervous, but as we would discover, you had a very expressive face. Viewed from the side, you always looked as though you were smiling, due to the way your mouth curved above your jaw line. In time I would get to know when you felt ultimately content, as you would half-close your eyes, in a slow-motion blink, while looking in my direction. I would respond in silence, narrowing my eyes to tell you I loved you and you would reflect the expression back to me, like a secret code between us.

At first you were incredibly shy, hiding away under furniture and recoiling from our attempts to interact with you. Gradually, you got used to your new surroundings, and in time you grew as attached to us as we became to you.

We treated you like a princess, keeping nowhere out of bounds, unlike the home you'd just come from. Jeanette hadn't allowed you upstairs in her house, or on the furniture, and she shut you in the dining room overnight. It mystified me how you'd coped with that life, since you were such an affectionate little thing who thrived on attention and company. You were welcome on our sofa, you loved my Papasan chair, and every night you slept with us on our bed.

Over our cat-sitting weekend, Craig and I asked ourselves what we would do in the unlikely event of Jeanette allowing us to keep you. It seemed like a hypothetical fantasy, but we knew the reality of owning a pet should be taken seriously. We weighed up the pros and cons and talked ourselves around in circles, unable to arrive at a firm decision. As much as you were an adorable little fluff-ball who was fun to have around, there would be the question of affording veterinary fees and cat food, being there to feed you twice a day, and cleaning out your litter tray. Not to mention finding care for you when we went on our own holidays. Anyway, it was a moot point, as you staying with us wasn't likely to be an option. Or so we thought.

Back at work that Saturday, you provided a fresh topic of conversation around the phone calls and filing.

'How's wee Molly?' Ally asked.

'She's gorgeous,' I replied. 'She's coming out of her shell and playing with us a little.'

'Aww! I bet you're falling in love with her!' said Linda.

'We are, we won't want to give her back next week!' I laughed.

On the Monday afternoon, I arrived into work to find Jeanette returned from her break.

'Hullo Amy, how are you? I've heard all about how much you've loved looking after Molly. I hope she's been behaving herself.'

'Yes, she's adorable, she's been no bother at all. Such a sweet little cat, it's been a pleasure to have her stay with us.'

'Well, if you want to keep her, you can.'

She said it so nonchalantly, I couldn't quite believe it.

'Oh! Really?'

'Aye. She doesne get much company at our house, we don't really have enough time to look after her.'

Later, when Jeanette had left for the day, my colleagues revelled in excitement.

'So, are you gonne keep her?'

'I'll have to think about it.'

'But you've gushed about her all weekend, you're not gonne say no, are you?'

'It's a big decision! Taking on a cat is a huge commitment. I need to talk it through with Craig first.'

The ladies clucked around like a brood of chickens, incredulous at my lack of immediate celebration at the opportunity to keep you forever. Although secretly thrilled, I wanted to reserve my excitement until I'd confirmed with Craig what we wanted to do.

He was, of course, elated. Not just for an excuse to have a cat, but that we could give you a much happier life than you appeared to have had at Jeanette's house. When faced with the ultimate decision, we couldn't bear to send you back to a less loving home than ours.

When I had initially taken you home on the Thursday afternoon, Jeanette hadn't given me any information about you, your history or your needs. It turned out you had belonged to her boyfriend, although by the sounds of it he hadn't owned you for very long himself. His children had wanted him to get a cat, but the novelty had since worn off and they had grown less interested in you on their weekend visits. Since he worked a lot it seemed that none of them had found the time to become very attached to you, although goodness knows how, as to me, you were irresistibly lovable. I got the impression Jeanette wasn't much of a cat person, hence her indifference to your presence in her home.

You had a string of imperfections Craig and I found mildly concerning, but equally rather endearing. It quickly became apparent that your eyes didn't work as well as they should, as you often lost sight of your toys when we were playing with you. Your meow was timid and raspy, as if strained through a permanently sore throat or damaged vocal cords. In contrast, though, you had a warm, happy purr that melted our hearts.

When you walked, your left hip tended to click, indicating a historic accident or fracture. Often you would sit with your back leg jutting out at an odd angle, and you would need to rest it if you'd been walking around for a while.

All we knew about you for sure was that you were four or five years old and your name was Molly. When we went on holiday the following year, and left you in the care of our friend Tam, I produced a full page of typed A4, detailing comprehensive instructions and Molly-care information, so he could look after you properly. Quite a contrast to the muted hand-over we'd had from Jeanette on the day we met you.

It took weeks - no, actually - months, for you to build your trust in us. It was worth the wait though, as you turned out to be such a giving and affectionate pet. You were the most adorable little cat I'd ever seen, with your soft features and velvety fur. Your slight frame made you look more like a kitten than an adult cat. Even in your old age, you were still a kitten to me.

You enjoyed time on your own, as most cats do, frequently hiding from us in secret spaces you thought we wouldn't discover. One of your favourite spots was on the floor beside our bed. It was a low-set, solid Ikea bed, with an MDF base and a six-inch wide lip providing an edge around the sunk mattress. On one side, it butted up to the wall, creating a shelter underneath, which you would crawl along and take refuge in. The only way I could spot you there was by sitting on the surround with my bony bum resting half on the mattress, half on the hard edge, pressing my face firmly against the cold wall and squinting down through the slim gap to spot a flash of your white fur.

One afternoon I realised it had been a couple of hours since I'd seen you last. I searched all the usual places several times, growing increasingly worried, but adamant there was no way you could have wandered out of the flat. Satisfied you weren't in any other nooks or crannies, I lay splayed out on the kitchen floor, shining a torch under the units, calling and calling your name to entice you out. After several minutes, flustered cheek pressed against cold lino, I heard a noise by the door and shuffled around to see you casually saunter in, looking at me as if I'd lost the plot.

Every morning, without fail, you would wake us up for breakfast. Your meal times were seven a.m. and six p.m. However, when you woke us at six thirty a.m., crying, walking over us and treading on our faces, we would soon give in and feed you early. Breakfast time gradually became earlier and earlier, until I was getting up at five a.m. to feed you, just to stop your incessant crying. We tried giving you a little extra food when we went to bed, at eleven p.m. or midnight, in the hope you wouldn't be hungry for breakfast at an ungodly hour the next day. It didn't work, though. You still woke us at five a.m., or earlier, asking to be fed again. In the end we just had to be strict, not give in to you before the crack of dawn, and stick to the original plan. It wasn't easy for any of us, but eventually you accepted the set routine.

The summer after you came to Sandbank Crescent brought some beautifully sunny days, and we would open most of the windows in the flat to allow fresh air to breeze through. On one particular stiflingly hot day, Craig walked into the living room to find you on the wrong side of the glass. You had jumped out of the small top window and landed on the external sill, sitting one floor above ground level, casually sniffing the air. You had gone in search of some respite from the oppressive heat indoors, but you appeared to be completely oblivious to the danger in which you were putting yourself. Without thinking, Craig dropped what he was carrying and bolted across the room, reaching out of the window to gather you back in. Thankfully, he was tall and slim, with arms long enough to reach you. You weren't at all scared and, due to your poor eyesight, probably had no idea of the drop, inches from your paws.

You were incredibly playful and loved an opportunity for a game. Any toy, any time, provided hours of pure pleasure. One day, when Craig's friend Colin was visiting, we were all in the living room chilling out and chatting. Colin was sitting on the sofa, mindlessly drumming his fingers on the end of the armrest, while engrossed in conversation. Unbeknownst to us, you caught sight of the movement and thought he was playing a game. Having spotted the prey, you stalked the moving digits from the doorway, silently creeping across the carpet in stealth mode. Then you leapt up to grab the living toy, sinking your sharp claws into Colin's fingers and giving him the fright of his life! He learned a valuable lesson that day and consciously sat on his hands whenever he came back to visit.

On the whole, you were very careful when playing with us in close contact. We got you some catnip, which you loved. I'd rub my fingers in the bag and extend my hand towards you. Intrigued, you would sniff the digits, then paw at them. Then, being careful not to grip too hard with your claws, you'd pull my hand to your mouth before chewing at my fingertips, ever so lightly and gently so as not to hurt me, while reaping the benefit of the feline narcotic.

Craig regularly travelled north into the wilds of Scotland to find the best locations to photograph. On one occasion, he returned with some large buzzard tail feathers. The scent of them entranced you, sending you into a frenzy, clawing and chewing at them as he danced them above your head. He attached them to the top of your scratching post so you could hunt them any time you liked. Craig made it his mission to always return home from his adventures with fresh feathers for you to play with.

Another game you loved was at bedtime, when we had our hands under the bedclothes and tapped upwards to create bumps, which you would pounce on, like a 'whack-a-mole' game. We had hours of fun playing that until late into the night. You didn't like being under the covers yourself, unless we held them up to create a den. A bed-cave was always warm and cosy, but you didn't like the quilt resting on top of your body. I would open up a space for you to get comfy in and support the duvet roof with my arm or leg, holding it until my limb ached. Eventually I would need to submit and collapse the cave on top of you. Within seconds, you would indignantly crawl out and settle back on top of the covers. The only exception to this was in the coldest of winters later on, when I could gently cover you with a light blanket.

Most days, you had a mad twenty minutes when you would tear around the flat with terrific energy before collapsing on the floor in sheer exhaustion. Since your eyesight wasn't brilliant, you would occasionally run across the room at full-pelt, straight into a table leg or door frame. Shocked, and worried that you'd done yourself some serious damage, my concern quickly dissipated, as you walked away nonchalantly with your head held high as if to say, "I didn't do that ... No, no, nothing to see here." I always proclaimed that I thought you had a skull of steel, since throughout your life people would comment on how unfazed you were by walking – or running – head first into solid objects.

For a while I had the idea of filming your daft exploits, and in hindsight I regret that I didn't. This was back in the very early days of YouTube, before the conception of camera phones. Craig had a camcorder, but I wasn't inclined to use it. I felt reluctant to exploit your disability for the entertainment of others. If I had, though, I think you would have had a very popular channel.

CHAPTER TWO: The Great Outdoors

'Of all God's creatures, there is only one that cannot be made slave of the leash. That one is the cat.'

— *Mark Twain*

Once settled into your new home with us, you became curious about what was on the other side of the front door, through which we would disappear every day for hours at a time. It felt mean to keep you confined indoors and stifle your curiosity, so we decided to let you explore a little. I opened the door, and you tentatively ventured out to the communal hallway. The space was a carpeted three metre by three metre square, with a front-facing window to the left and our neighbour's front door opposite ours. On the right, a set of stairs disappeared up to the top floor, and further along the landing more stairs lead down to ground level.

You had a good sniff around for about ten minutes, before retreating to the familiarity of the flat. You were a timid little thing; your curiosity balanced out by your cautiousness. Having limited eyesight restricted your confidence, but it didn't dampen your instinct to explore. Each day, we would take a walk out of the flat, and you would venture a little further than the last. Your first milestone was the top of the stairs that lead to the ground floor. I encouraged you along by leading the way and talking to you, to reassure you it was safe. You dropped down each stair in turn, sniffing and exploring every surface as you went. It was a few days before you reached the half-way landing area, and a few more after that, the bottom of the stairwell. Next to investigate was the ground floor hallway (or, I should say, 'the close': you were a Scottish cat, after all) and then along to the front door of our modest block of flats.

The block was home to six apartments; two on each floor. Our neighbours were all professional adults, and we rarely heard or crossed paths with them. I was glad none of them opened their doors while we were exploring, since it would have taken some explaining why I was guiding my cat around the building. It probably would have scared you too, and I didn't want anything to deter you from your adventures. Over the weeks, we made our way to the main front door, and once there, I stood holding it open, waiting patiently to see if you would muster the courage to step outside. Eventually you did, and the quiet cul-de-sac of Sandbank Crescent became your new exploration site.

There were four blocks of flats on our side of the road. The opposite south side was lined with houses, ranging in size from bungalows at the top through to large family homes at the secluded end, all in the same red brick design, with dark brown tiled roofs. The canal was hidden from our view, sitting stagnant at the bottom of the private gardens, emerging from behind the first bungalow and sweeping off on its course, while the road curved away, up to the main Sandbank Street.

Craig and I had a running joke about the potential to spend our whole adult lives living on the Crescent. Looking out across the road, it felt like a life goal to get on the property ladder with a small house opposite, and then gradually up-size along to the end. Probably followed by down-sizing back to a bungalow in retirement.

Few of the neighbours in the flats and houses on our small cul-de-sac knew each other, but we began to break that mould as people started to recognise me as 'the girl who walks the cat'. You were very popular. No-one could resist cooing over and petting such an adorable little creature. The year before we left Glasgow, I organised a summer street party to generate some community spirit. It was a wonderful day, although you weren't comfortable around so many people, so you soon returned indoors. No doubt you overheard the frivolities while curled up in the Papasan chair, appreciating the comfort and solitude of home.

The idea of getting you a lead or harness for our walks never crossed my mind. You wouldn't roam much further than the limit of your last outing, and you were always obedient when I needed to enforce boundaries.

At the top of the crescent, on the right-hand side, was an Orange Hall*,[1] and then a junction with the busier Sandbank Street. You were brave enough to venture right up past the white concrete building, but when you got near the road, I would gently and sternly call your name, and you knew exactly what I meant. I also knew exactly what you meant with your responding scratchy meows. Our arguments went something like this:

'Molly, no, you're not allowed over there!'

(You stopped and cried) 'Oh, but I just want to go a little further!'

'No, the road is up there and it's dangerous. You're not allowed to go up that far.'

(Still not moving, but objecting) 'Go on, please! I want to see what's there. I bet it's exciting!'

'Come on now, come back this way. It's too dangerous and I might lose you.'

(Conceding and turning back towards me) 'Ohhh okay. But I really want to explore up there.'

---

1 *Orange Halls, or Lodges, are meeting places for members of the Orange Order; a protestant fraternity based in Northern Ireland, with a strong presence in Scotland. They hold Orange Walks throughout the summer, their parades through Glasgow City centre including brass bands, one of which regularly rehearsed at the Hall at the end of Sandbank Crescent.

We had a few of these discussions in different parts of the crescent: by the copse of trees I didn't want you to get lost in, next to the fence alongside the main road, and approaching the bank of the canal, where it briefly kissed the corner of the street. Most of our conversations were short. Occasionally they would go on for a few minutes, but only a handful of times did I have to resort to picking you up and pointing you in a safer direction. I trusted you and it paid off. You trusted me back and our friendship deepened.

There were times we were outside for more than half an hour and I would be anxious to get back indoors and do some work, or at least something a little more productive than hanging about on the street. However, I felt mean taking you back in before you were ready, so usually I gave you as much time as you wanted. Having said that, you seemed to know instinctively when I didn't have time to spare and I was grateful on the days you only wanted a brief stroll around. I was also very grateful that you disliked the rain, or wet paving slabs, so I was never stuck outside in miserable weather waiting for you.

Introducing you to snow was amusing, but also rather sad, as you didn't understand what it was. Arriving at the front door, you stepped over the threshold, excited for your walk. Then, plunging your paw into several inches of soft, cold flakes, you jumped straight back inside, your reaction saying, 'What on earth is this!? What have you done to my lovely outdoors? I can't walk in this!' You may have tried it once or twice, but you hated it and would reluctantly return to the warm, dry flat.

When I was running short of time and keen to get back, I would carry you up the stairs. Otherwise, I would close the main front door and wait patiently for you to make your own way up to the flat. Sometimes I'd go ahead, propping open our door so I could get on with my day until you were safely back inside. Even then, I would keep popping out to check on your progress, in case you got lost or tried to head back outdoors. It was unlikely someone else would come along and accidentally let you out. Once or twice you continued up the stairs and found yourself by a neighbour's door, thinking it was ours. Thankfully Caroline, who lived above us, was lovely, and had a soft spot for you. The chap who lived opposite her kept himself to himself, and we never saw him enter or leave.

In the three years we lived together in Glasgow, you successfully made it all the way around the crescent, sniffing at every front door and exploring up and down the grassy banks in between and behind the blocks of flats. We occasionally crossed paths with the odd neighbourhood pet, and it quickly became clear you were not fond of other animals. I didn't expect you to get along with dogs, but you wouldn't tolerate other cats either. You were an only child and you wouldn't have it any other way.

Most cats kept their distance, but one or two wanted to meet you, and there was a beautiful Bengal kitty who was quite persistent. You'd be blissfully unaware of his presence until he was close enough for you to catch his scent, at which point you would become perturbed and hiss. It was the only time I ever saw you being aggressive, although I knew you were acting out of fear rather than anger. I would have loved for you to have made some feline friends, especially when they approached you with purely curious and friendly intentions. It wasn't to be though, so I learned to shoo them away so you wouldn't freak out and run off, literally in a blind panic, losing all sense of direction.

For a brief time, you fancied yourself as a bird catcher. Natural for most cats, of course, but due to your limited eyesight it was never going to be a skill you would master. On one of our walks, you became aware of some young birds flying around above us and diving towards the ground for food. Your senses piqued and your eyes shone, as if you thought you might catch one as it swooped. Sadly for you, your eyes couldn't communicate with your brain fast enough to time a successful attack. Despite your failure, and quietly grateful I didn't have to witness success, I did love watching your excitement at the prospect of catching a bird.

The only danger you faced outside, apart from getting lost, was of getting run over. You loved cars - especially moving ones. If a vehicle arrived into the crescent, you would head towards it rather than run away, and on numerous occasions I had to pick you up when I heard an approaching engine. Cars appealed to you because they were warm when recently parked, so you enjoyed sitting underneath them, sheltered from the elements.

One time, I was in my own little world while you were relaxing under a car, until I began to feel rather self-conscious. Any curtain-twitchers who weren't familiar with our walks would have wondered why I was hanging about on the pavement with no apparent purpose; especially if they were the owner of the vehicle I was loitering near. I liked to think I didn't resemble your typical car thief or miscreant, but I did wonder what people would think. I often took a book out with me, so I would look busy, but then why would someone be casually reading a book while standing on a residential street? There were grassy lawns in front of the flats, but being so public, they weren't the kind of gardens you would sit in for an afternoon. Besides which, I needed to watch you carefully, which meant following you around on your walks.

Twenty minutes or so went by and my patience began to wane, so I made my way over to the car to see what you were doing under there. I was determined that our walks were for walking rather than for sitting around, which was just as easily achieved indoors. I stooped down with the intention of encouraging you out. You were sitting beside a wheel, holding your gaze purposefully towards the other side of the car. I followed your stare and saw, by the tyre on the other side, a large dead blackbird. You weren't attempting to eat it, touch it, or even approach it, but you had a look in your eye that said with a great deal of pride, "I killed that!" That was the closest you ever came, certainly in the years I knew you, to successful hunting.

As your sight gradually deteriorated, I opted to wear hard-soled or heeled shoes on our walks, so you could hear my footsteps and always know where I was, since you would panic if you thought you had lost me. While you followed the sound of my feet on the pavement, I also made other noises, sucking in air through my teeth, or clicking my tongue, to guide you towards me or reassure you I was close by. If I became bored and wanted to go back indoors without completely cutting short our walk and carrying you, I would slowly head back towards the flat, hoping you would follow the guiding sound of my footsteps. It didn't always work. If you wanted longer outside, you would stand your ground or keep walking in the direction you were headed, making your objections clear. Once or twice I left you to walk on your own and make it back to our front door without me, which you managed with no problems, but I was never far away, checking you were safe.

Most outdoor cats also go to the toilet outside. I had assumed it was a natural instinct to use soil to do your business in, but for you this was not the case. You wouldn't go anywhere other than your litter tray, presumably because you had been trained that way. Without fail, you would go at least next to your toilet, if not exactly in it. You had a habit of walking around in the litter, doing a couple of tiny circuits of the tray, before backing up and sticking your bum just over the edge, before doing a number two. It would have been more amusing if I hadn't had to clean it up afterwards.

We bought a small wooden table with two solid sides that the tray fitted under perfectly. With its back end wedged up against the bathroom wall, we thought we'd solved the problem, but you still managed to do your business over the front. I had hoped that, once outdoors, you might discover a natural urge to go to the loo out there, but it wasn't to be. When you wanted to go out, you would head to the front door and look longingly at it, and then go to the bathroom and use the litter tray, before returning to the front door and looking at me as if to say, 'I'm a good girl, I've been to the loo… can I go outside now, please?'

On a trip to a vet for a general check-over, I was told you were fit and healthy, apart from a slightly irregular heartbeat. I wasn't sure whether to take that information with a pinch of salt, since I trust vets as much as I trust mechanics (i.e. with a certain level of wariness), but there was nothing that could be done about it in any case. I just had to hope it wouldn't stop you from living a full and happy life. As for your eyesight, there appeared to be no logical explanation for the loss, apart from 'just one of those things'. I had people telling me white cats often to go blind, but in fact white cats with blue eyes have a genetic tendency to go deaf. You had green eyes, but it didn't stop you from adopting selective hearing later on in life.

CHAPTER THREE:
Call Of The Wild

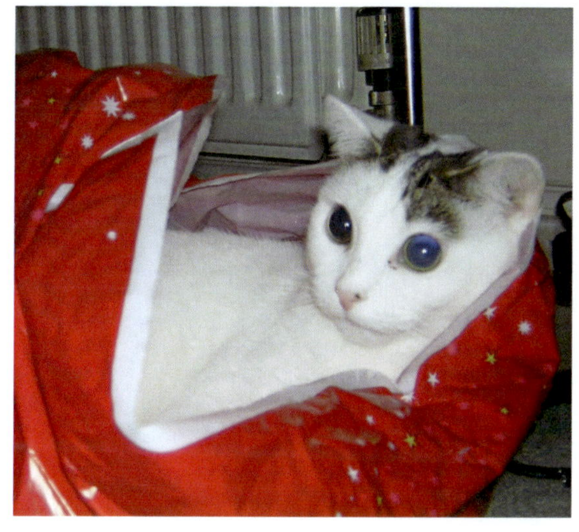

'Women and cats will do as they please, and men and dogs should relax and get used to the idea.'

— Robert A. Heinlein

All cats have their preferences when it comes to food, and I quickly learned you weren't a big fan of fish – whether in cat food or fresh – with the exception of tuna. This suited me, as we shared the same tastes. You had a disappointing lack of interest in Marmite, but you did, however, like me, enjoy dairy and meat of almost any variety. Later on I would find that, having got used to finishing the milk from my morning bowl of cereal, you'd turn your nose up at the white stuff fresh from the fridge, preferring the warmer, sweeter leftovers from my breakfast. I was aware cow's milk isn't meant to be good for cats to drink, but you loved it and it didn't seem to do you any harm, so I decided not to deny you the odd dairy treat.*[2]

To our fascination, Craig and I discovered that fresh meat brought out an instinctive wild-cat side of you. Whether taken from your bowl or from one of our plates or hands, you would walk around with the chunk in your mouth, making a cat-call that I can only describe as feral. At first we panicked that something was terribly wrong. You sounded in pain! However, we soon realised you were calling out to tell us you had found meat, as if you'd hunted it yourself to provide for your family. The noise was like a wild howl. The closest I can get to spelling it out would be "A-Aow, A-A-Aoww!" As part of this ritual, you would bring the food into the same room as us, if it wasn't already, and after much fuss and commotion you would let it drop to the floor.

Sometimes I tried to put an end to your loud vocalising, by saying, 'Well done, Molly, you've found some meat! Good girl!' Only when you were sure you had got your point across would you finally stop to devour it. Gripping the morsel with your

---

2 *Incidentally, I've cringed reading this back in 2020, as I no longer drink cow's milk, for health and ethical reasons, so I wouldn't advocate it!

claws on the carpet, you would tear at it with your teeth with a great deal of theatricality. You did this every time I gave you scraps of chicken or steak, almost without fail, throughout your life.

Whenever I cooked meat, I made sure to set aside a couple of pieces for you. We had a local butcher round the corner on Maryhill Road that I often visited. One Christmas, which Craig and I were spending on our own with you, we decided to treat ourselves to steak for our festive meal. I asked the butcher for large enough cuts of sirloin for two adults and a small cat. He clearly wasn't a pet person.

'Steak for your cat? What a waste of good meat!' He still took my money, though.

As far as I was concerned, as an important family member, you should have just as fine a Christmas dinner as us. (Don't worry, readers, we didn't go as far as giving her all the trimmings. Even I wouldn't waste a Yorkshire pudding on a cat!)

You kept your claws in top condition by using your scratching post. As a result, any piece of meat you clawed at became skewered on a pin-sharp talon, hindering your ability to wolf it down. With a flick (or three) of your paw, the morsel would release, but often you would then crouch down to eat, only to find it had disappeared. Unbeknownst to you, it had gone flying across the room. Unable to track it with your flawed eyesight, you were left utterly bewildered. Most of the time, Craig or I could retrieve the treat, or guide you to it, but if we hadn't witnessed the food fling, you would resign yourself to the loss. Later that day, or sometime the next, while padding barefoot around the flat, I would get an unwelcome surprise of a lump of cold meat squishing between my toes.

Several times a day you practised your scratching post ritual: a full-body stretch and good clawing session. The furniture and carpets were spared of being ripped apart, which I was immensely grateful for. Presumably this behaviour was instilled in you from an early age, although it was another habit you didn't transfer to the great outdoors, as you never attempted to scratch at, or climb, any trees. We had struggled to find a suitable scratching post for you, as back in those days, the only option in the shops was a single post, just over a foot tall. It made little sense that a fully grown cat, even a small one like you, should be expected to fulfil their claw-sharpening needs on apparatus so limited in height. You needed to reach up and grab at a high point in order to gain a proper purchase, flex all your muscles and use up excess energy. The solution Craig came up with was to buy two scratching posts, remove one from its base and butcher the remaining parts together, making a tower tall enough to allow you to achieve a decent stretch. It looked rather odd, but it did the job. We kept that quirky post for years, eventually replacing it with a large cat tree with platforms. These days there are so many options for cat furniture, I'm sorely tempted to decorate my house with high-level runs, ladders, and hammocks.

On the subject of furniture, despite enjoying time on the sofa and sleeping on our bed at night, your preference for a snoozing spot was always a cardboard box. Whenever a delivery arrived, I would be excited by the contents, while you'd be far more interested in the packaging; jumping straight in and making yourself comfortable. No box was too small for your slight frame. You were also partial to a plastic bag, as can be seen in the photo accompanying this chapter.

Another regular haunt of yours was the square wicker rubbish basket in the sitting room. Although larger than your preferred boxes, it provided much entertainment, as the gaps on each side that formed handles could be used as peep-holes (because as far as you were concerned you were concealed, despite the top being open). As you looked out from your secret hide, keeping watch for any interesting activity, we would drop a toy in front of the spy-hole and dangle it roughly within your reach. A paw would come darting out - swipe, swipe swipe - taking the prey by surprise. If you caught it, it would vanish into the hole, to be kept as a proudly fawned-over trophy.

When you weren't cat-napping in a nook, you were usually seeking attention, interrupting anything I might be doing. I would pick a quiet moment to practise yoga, but you always seemed to know when I was laying out my mat, and you were fascinated by my strange shapes. Being skilled yourself in the aptly named downward-dog and cat-cow poses, it was surprising you thought it so strange that I partook in my own stretching routine. You would weave in and out of my arms and legs, settle by my feet or curl up right under my face, preventing me from stepping through to a sun salutation. Far from being irritated, I found it cute and would end up collapsing into giggles before giving up, aiming to try again during your next snooze.

The only other significant memory I have from our time in Glasgow is how you would react to arguments. Craig and I rarely fell out, but when we did, it got heated and loud. I recall you coming into the room and crying at us, as if you were trying to break up the row. When that didn't work, you attempted to distract me by asking for attention and climbing up my leg, or sitting on my lap. Or perhaps you were looking for comfort in the frosty atmosphere. Either way, the argument would end and I'd reassure you everything was okay again.

Our relationship was far from tempestuous, but it wasn't without its faults, and Craig and I split up for good in the autumn of 2006. The only practical option for your residence was to stay with me in the flat while he moved back to his parents' house. His family's two cats were still living there, so you going with him wasn't a viable solution. It was heartbreaking for Craig to leave you and he missed you a great deal, but I can't deny how happy it made me that I won your custody. Or perhaps it would be more apt to say that you won mine.

My friend Kat moved in with us, and by then I had reignited my career in stage management. It took me off on tour, sometimes disappearing for weeks at a time; often rehearsing in London, and then travelling anywhere from the rural wilds of Wales to the converted desert of Dubai. Every time I started a new job I felt bad about leaving, but I trusted Kat to take care of you, being an animal person herself. When I returned from my trips, you were grumpy with me for a couple of days, putting me in the proverbial dog-house for abandoning you. However, you would soon forgive me and things would return to normal, until my next job away from home.

Kat had a guinea pig, and I was a little nervous about how you would react to it, since our experiences of other animals outside the flat had been wholly negative. However, to my relief, you were apathetic about its existence. You would sniff it out of curiosity, when it was shuffling about on the living room floor, but you neither particularly disliked it nor wanted to play with it, and its feelings appeared to be mutual.

CHAPTER FOUR: Malvern, 2007

'Never try to outstubborn a cat.'

— *Robert A. Heinlein, Time Enough for Love*

The beginning of Summer 2007 heralded time to leave Glasgow. As much as I loved living in Scotland, I wanted to be closer to my family and work. I had a three-month tour that was due to rehearse in London, so it made sense to move my belongings to my dad's house for a while. Working in theatre can be economically challenging when paying rent or a mortgage for a home you barely see, on top of digs while you're away. Traditionally, producers didn't pay for rehearsals, only for performances, and occasionally this was still the case when I was working in the industry. These days companies should provide touring expenses, but with most productions lucky to break even, stage work rarely comes with a generous financial reward.

My father lived in Malvern, in the West Midlands, not far from the Welsh border. The small town is famous for its beautiful rolling hills and fresh spring water. Whilst not a location commutable to London, Dad could look after you while I worked away. The move would be your biggest upheaval and change of lifestyle in all our time together.

The journey from Glasgow to Malvern was epic, and not in a good way. We had hired a transit van, which Dad drove while I held you on my lap in your travel box. The carrier was a blue plastic crate with a yellow metal grill door, and you absolutely hated being in it. The addition of a newspaper floor and some familiar-smelling toys did nothing to ease your distress. We had established that you didn't enjoy travelling when I'd previously driven you to the vet's, and you'd cried the entire time we were moving. You weren't agitated when the car was stationary; even stopped briefly at traffic lights you would settle down, but as soon as we moved again, you became inconsolable.

The drive to Dad's took around six hours, and you were desperate to get out of the carrier from the moment we left. After a while, I thought you might be calmer if you weren't so confined and had access to my lap. I turned the box on my knees so the door was facing towards me and released the latches to allow you a little freedom. As soon as the opportunity arose, you were out and climbing on me. You settled for a while, although you were still stressed; your breathing shallow and rapid, your pupils dilated; each one a great eclipse, surrounded by a white corona flare.

At times, your mouth opened wide, and you started panting. Your facial muscles were so tense your jaw locked open and you looked increasingly distressed. I talked to you constantly and stroked you, trying to calm you down. That helped for a few minutes, but then you reverted to wide-mouthed panting again. It was horrible, but there was nothing more I could do.

A couple of hours into the journey, we stopped at a service station so Dad and I could get some breakfast. After returning you to the carrier, I left you on the seat, telling you we wouldn't be long. I was worried about leaving you, but we made sure there was enough ventilation and I figured that, being stationary, you might settle.

When we got back less than half an hour later, you were wandering around the cab – somehow you had managed to break out of the box. I couldn't work out how you'd done it. There was no obvious damage, and I had definitely secured the door shut. You must have bust the metal grill out of its clasps through sheer determination, although I do enjoy the idea of you calmly turning the two plastic latches with a claw, before gently pushing it free and stepping outside.

We put some water in a dish and let you out onto the nearby grass, but it didn't make you any happier, as your surroundings were so unfamiliar. We spent the rest of the journey with you partly on my lap and partly investigating the van, sniffing around every bit of the confined space you could access. Once you had exhausted my side of the cab, you climbed over towards the driver's footwell.

'Molly, no! You can't go down there, it's very dangerous. Stay on my lap with me.' This time, although I'm sure you understood what I was saying, you weren't interested in listening, or obeying. I tried to keep hold of you, but you kept wriggling free and arguing back, determined to have your way.

'You've taken me out of my home and brought me to this strange place, I demand to know where I am. LET. ME. GO!'

'Maybe we should let her explore,' said Dad. 'She's calmer when she's sniffing about, and it's probably less dangerous than you fishing around my feet trying to grab her.'

And so it was that we left you to your own devices. You explored every nook and cranny, before emerging in your own time and taking solace back on my lap. You stayed there for the rest of the journey, albeit in varying degrees of distress.

Over the following few months my father looked after you and treated you with all the love and care you deserved, but living with him wasn't exactly the happiest period of your life. Dad shared a house with his elderly mother. He had the upstairs to himself while my granny lived downstairs, with two cats of her own. I was concerned with how the arrangement would work for you, but since the other cats didn't go upstairs and you were used to living on one floor, being confined to what was effectively a flat shouldn't have been much of a problem.

Despite the complete change in your surroundings, which came with unfamiliar smells and company, you settled in as best you could and found some cosy spots to make your own.

Dad tried to encourage you downstairs occasionally, for some fresh air out in the garden. You would reach the ground-floor hallway, but as soon as you caught the scent of the other cats you became stressed and rushed back upstairs to the safety of your newly established territory. You never made it outdoors while you lived there. I didn't like the idea of carrying you outside because I knew you would feel disorientated, which would cause you extra anxiety and probably prevent you from being able to enjoy the garden at all.

Granny would sometimes go upstairs to talk to you, but she must have smelled of her cats, because whenever she got near, your hackles shot up and you hissed at her until she went away again. My poor elderly grandmother got the impression you didn't like her at all. Even when she came to visit us for Christmas several years later in London, you started hissing any time she approached you.

The only argument I ever had with my Granny was over a misunderstanding about you. When it came time to move again, I was having a discussion with Dad about your care, and wanting to prioritise your welfare. I'm not sure what she overheard, but she became very distressed and upset with me. It turned out she thought I was talking about having you put down, as I couldn't look after you properly. That was the last thing that would ever have crossed my mind.

I once came across an article online in which someone was asking for advice on what to do about their cat, who was going blind. I was appalled to read stories of people who'd had their pets put to sleep because of their impaired eyesight. We were incredibly lucky that you could still function so well, despite your disability. Other cats ended up with no life at all, completely debilitated and no longer able to find their food or litter tray, or make their way around their homes.

After calming Granny down, I gently explained that she'd misunderstood my intentions, and you'd be coming with me when I moved.

During your time at my dad's, you developed a small lump on your lower back, an inch from your spine, at the top of a brown tabby patch. Luckily, the local veterinary practice was just across the road, and were able to reassure Dad it wasn't cancerous. The growth was a benign cyst, so they drained the fluid away with a needle. Unfortunately, that wasn't the end of it, as the lump reappeared, and every so often I'd need to take you to have it syringed.

After nine months based in Malvern, with an opera tour, a Panto, and a Lorca play added to my CV, I secured a long-term job in a regional theatre in Essex. So once again, we relocated. I found a house-share close to Colchester town centre, in Cromwell Road. Given how stressful the move from Glasgow had been, Dad and I sought advice from the vet, who gave us something to calm you for the journey. It worked. You were significantly more relaxed than you had been on the previous trip.

You were very happy in the new house. There was more space to explore and a garden you could enjoy without having to cross the territory of other cats. There had once been a cat flap in the back door, and the gap it left had since been boarded up. The live-in landlord, Giles, agreed to install a new flap, but initially he removed the ply board that covered the existing hole. It was spring, the weather was warm, and for the first time you had unhindered access to your own outdoor space.

Just as you had in Glasgow, you explored at your own pace, settling into the indoor surroundings before venturing outside. It didn't take you long though, and it helped that our bedroom was on the ground floor, so once again, for all intents and purposes, you were living in a flat. You spent some time sitting in the kitchen, by the hole in the back door, enjoying the fresh air breezing in, before building up the courage to step through to the wider world. Once you did, you loved it out there, especially as you then had the freedom to go out whenever you wanted. I still supervised you to begin with, but you weren't interested in roaming beyond the garden fence, you were happy enough lying in the grass, basking in the sounds and smells of nature.

After a month or so, Giles got around to installing a new cat flap, which thoroughly confused you. Your eyesight had deteriorated significantly over the previous couple of years, and you relied heavily on your whiskers to guide you past walls and furniture. You had quickly become accustomed to where everything was, but then, when you went to the garden door, there was no gap to go through. It had gone. Having never used a cat flap before, you didn't know you had to push it open, and it wasn't easy teaching you. Being as timid and as gentle as you were, you would never attempt to, quite literally, push your boundaries. If your whiskers found a solid surface, it wouldn't occur to you that you could move it. So, I would hold open the plastic door for you to feel the light breeze coming through, and then close and open it again, trying to help you understand. However, no matter how many times I demonstrated it, you still didn't realise you might be able to move it yourself. I had to pick you up and push you through the flap to demonstrate its potential. After a while, you started to get it. You would nudge it a little, feel the fresh air on your face, and just stand there for a while before retracting your head back into the kitchen. I was incredibly proud when you finally disappeared through it and, contrary to your fears, discovered you hadn't lost your freedom after all.

Life was good in Cromwell Road. It was a quiet, comfortable home, and I had the time and resources to revive my love of cooking, often making meals to share. As well as Giles, we lived with Lisa, a German girl. She was lovely, but none too impressed with the fur you left behind on the sofa, which would transfer onto her smart work clothes whenever she sat down. I'd grown used to it, especially as I almost exclusively wore black attire for my job, and it was near impossible to keep it from being coated in bright, contrasting hairs. I always had a supply of lint rollers to hand, although I would invariably leave the house covered in glowing white fluff and shed your fur myself, wherever I went.

Our room was at the front of the house. It was large, bright, and airy and had the added benefit of you not needing to use the stairs. However, your poor eyesight didn't hinder your curiosity and if Lisa left her bedroom door open on the first floor, we would often discover you fast asleep on her bed.

Our peaceful routine was interrupted when your toilet habits started going awry. You had never had any serious problems, beyond your bottom-aiming issues, but out of the blue you took to peeing on the floor, near the litter tray, instead of in it. I was mortified that you were weeing on Giles' lovely real-wood floor boards. I tried everything I could think of to break your new bad habit, from cleaning out the box more often than usual, to trying different types of litter, telling you off when you didn't use it, and putting you in the tray to remind you where to pee. Eventually you drifted back to your normal good behaviour and I could only put it down to an unfortunate, unsettled phase.

Thankfully, Giles was a very chilled out landlord and took it all in his stride. I'd bought you a covered litter tray when we moved in, which was a whole new advent in cat toilets at the time. The most convenient location for it was in the entrance hallway, near the front door, so the enclosed cubicle afforded you some privacy. It also helped to reduce the smells and unsightliness from our housemates and any visitors. And it had the added benefit of preventing you from being able to poo over the edge.

CHAPTER FIVE: Colchester, 2008

'The smallest feline is a masterpiece.'

— Leonardo da Vinci

Cromwell Road was our home for six months. While we were there, I met and dated Dean. He was handsome and kind, and we soon decided to move in together. We chose a two-bedroom, ground-floor flat nearby, on Hythe Hill. It was a busy main road, so we didn't let you out through the front door, but there was access to a shared garden at the back. The rear kitchen door opened out to a patio, then a set of concrete steps down to a lower level, with grassy banks on either side. A path at the bottom lead around to a gate, beyond which was a residents' car park. Our communal outdoor space was enclosed by neighbours on two sides, and fences and a bike shed on the others. The garden was big enough for your exploring, but impossible for you to get lost in.

There was no cat flap, so we had to let you out for supervised outdoor time. Although inconvenient when you'd got used to having your freedom, it meant you couldn't sneak out if the gate was left open, and end up in the car park, or beyond. Also, the garden not being private bore a risk of you getting scared by other residents and ending up disorientated. Thankfully, there weren't any other animals living in our block, which was one less thing to worry about, but there were several small children. I became friendly with our closest neighbour, Jade, who had a three-year-old son called Max. He had lots of energy, but was very good with you. Max wasn't your favourite person, but that didn't stop you snooping around their flat when you got a chance to sneak in, instigating games of hide-and-seek with an excitable toddler.

You quickly got used to Dean's company, and the two of you rubbed along together just fine. Moving house and living with new people didn't faze you. My presence provided a sense of security and you trusted those I brought into our lives. I think the ultimate sign of your acceptance of Dean was when he was lying in bed and you walked up his chest and started cleaning his beard. You licked and pulled at it until he giggled so much he had to move you away.

Dean also found it highly amusing to have conversations with you, because you always had to have the last word. Whenever he spoke to you, you'd respond, and no matter how long the discussion lasted, each comment would be punctuated with a raspy reply.

'Alright Molly, how's it going?'

'Meow.'

'Oh, really? What are your plans for today?'

'Meow.'

'Interesting. Well, I'm off to work now.'

'Meow.'

'I'll see you later.'

'Meow.'

'Bye.'

'Meow.'

'You can stop replying now.'

... 'Meow.'

You loved to join in when we were being sociable. You weren't keen on large groups, but you chose to be in the room if two or three people were around. Even if not on a lap, you'd be somewhere nearby, within a comfortable distance of company. I think you enjoyed the security of knowing you weren't alone.

Just as it had happened with Craig, if there was an argument, you would interrupt and attempt to diffuse it, but another scenario you would involve yourself in was when Dean and I were getting friendly in bed. Possibly interpreting the passionate soundtrack as conflict, you would jump up and walk over us, around us, and in between us, trying to get our attention. It was a regular passion killer.

One of my least favourite household chores was changing the bedsheets. It always took longer than it should have because whenever I had the time and inclination to do it, you would just happen to be curled up and comfortable on the bed. If not, you would soon be in the room, jumping up, looking for attention and wanting to join in, or choosing to have a nap where I was working. Doing as much as I could around you to avoid disturbing your peace, I would gently move you out of the way to continue the job. Naturally, you would then settle somewhere else on the mattress I had yet to work on.

Once the sheets were stripped, I had the challenge of fitting the fresh ones. Sometimes I would wait until you were busying yourself in another room, but often it would get to bed time before I'd had the chance to do it and there you would be, wanting to be on the bed, of course. It was a continual game of shifting you from one side of the mattress to the other – since lifting you off it completely was pointless, as you'd jump straight back on again. I'd pick you up and put you down on the other side, or on the floor, but you would immediately reappear in the same space I needed to lay the sheet.

It was in that flat on Hythe Hill I have a residing memory of you being your most annoying. It was possibly the only time you ever really made me angry. You'd never had any particularly bad habits, other than the toilet issue. There was no danger of you bringing dead animals into the house, and you were generally unassuming and well-behaved. However, you went through phases of keeping me awake at night; walking all over me and crying for attention. Instead of giving in and petting you, I was determined to teach you that it wasn't okay to wake me up at all hours. I adopted the same technique I'd used to put a stop to you waking me up stupidly early for breakfast, but this time ignoring you didn't work, so I had to try a different approach. I would give you a little fuss, hoping you'd settle back down, but it was never enough. You were persistent and often refused to leave me alone, even if I did pet you for a while. As far as I could tell, there was nothing wrong – you weren't poorly or distressed – it was just a phase of behaviour when our body clocks were completely out of sync. Sometimes you would wake me up and quickly settle again. Other times, you wouldn't stop until you had my full conscious attention, which, over time, was exhausting.

I don't think you ever really grasped the human sleep pattern, or understood that it was different from yours. Even when you were older and you slept more, you rarely napped for longer than a few hours at a time. I am not a morning person. It takes me a good twenty minutes, at least, to feel vaguely alive. By contrast, it took you only twenty seconds to transition from fast asleep to wide awake, with a bit of cat-yoga in between. So, when your demands for attention in the middle of the night were met with groggy groans, I think you were quite offended. Waking you up from the depths of peaceful slumber didn't seem to bother you, so I discovered it was fruitless trying to show you how annoying it was by giving you a taste of your own medicine. How deeply unfair it is that a cat can curl up wherever and whenever it likes and then emerge from deep sleep, straight to full consciousness, with no struggle in between.

We tried shutting you out of the bedroom when we turned in, to stop you disturbing us through the night, but we'd wake to the sound of you scratching at the door and tearing up the carpet. I decided I valued our rental deposit more than my sleep, so that new rule was abandoned rather quickly, followed by some amateur carpet repair.

I would wake to the weight of your small feet carefully and tentatively padding up my legs, measuring their balance as they tested out the uneven surface under the duvet. You found your footing over the terrain of my body, padding all the way up to my head, before nuzzling your face into mine and tickling me with your whiskers and your cold, damp nose. I'd push you away, saying, 'No, Molly, I'm sleeping!' Moments later, you would creep back up to my face again. I would push you away, moving you further down the bed and turning you around, hoping you would continue forwards and settle by my feet. It didn't work. You just came back. You knew I wasn't happy with you, but you'd keep taking your chances. By this point I would be awake and watching you, as it turned into a game reminiscent of the school playground classic, 'What's the time, Mr Wolf?' You'd creep towards my head with a pitiful look in your eyes, freezing when you heard or felt me move, and waiting until you thought it was safe to continue. If you made it right up to my face, I'd push you back down the bed and the game would begin all over again. This sometimes went on for an unreasonably long time, before you would finally give up and lie down. You wouldn't gain my affections, but you would rouse me to full consciousness, so I'd find myself fully alert just as you were settling down to sleep.

In retrospect it's amusing, but at the time it was incredibly irritating. I imagined it would be like having a baby who needed feeding at all hours, although I'd not had that experience to compare it with, and I certainly got no maternity leave to compensate. The worst times were when you kept me awake all through the night. I would eventually get up in the morning, feed you and get ready for work, exhausted and sleep-deprived. After breakfast, you would curl up somewhere and fall fast asleep, without a care in the world, while I had to go to work, bleary-eyed and frazzled.

I tried hard to stay resolute over not giving you attention at night, as I didn't want the habit to stick. However, you often won over my heart. My infuriation reached boiling point while you kept me awake, but then one look at your irresistible furry little face would melt me into submission, and instantly all would be forgiven. I'd inevitably end up showering you with the love and affection you craved.

There was one exception to this. You woke me at about four a.m. and wouldn't leave me alone. You cried and cried, walking all over me, determined to win my attention. No matter how many times I shooed you away and pushed you to the bottom of the bed, you came back meowing and pawing at me. I felt as though I was going mad, being subjected to this torture when I desperately needed to sleep. Exasperated, I picked you up with my right hand and threw you to the end of the bed. You gripped on with your claws and left painful scratches all the way down my arm, hand, and fingers, before landing on the edge of the mattress and then falling to the floor. You got the message and retired to another room while I nursed my wounds and tried to sleep, my head and heart filled with an awful sense of guilt, mixed with quiet relief.

Your habit of keeping your claws sharp meant scratches

appeared easily on my arms, chest, and face when you walked over me at night. And since your eyesight was fading, you gripped on extra tight when walking over uneven surfaces, to help you balance. Every time I picked you up, you attached yourself to my arm, chest, or shoulder, as if your life depended on it.

I also suffered puncture wounds to my stomach, where you insisted on paddy-pawing: an addiction that sent you into a trance. Your big wide eyes stared into space as if you were having an otherworldly experience, your paws rhythmically kneading my belly, claws extending and retracting with every movement. I attempted to reduce the extent of the pain you were inflicting on me by moving your feet with my fingers, unpinning your spiky nails from my clothes and flesh. This act was not just a habit, it seemed to be a baser instinct – a task you had to complete in order to fulfil your feline duties. As much as it was painful for me, I never scolded you for it, as it was clearly an intrinsic need and a source of comfort.

There are three theories for the origin of this behaviour, referred to by some as 'making biscuits', due to the similarity to the action required for kneading the dough. The first school of thought is that it's simply an act of marking your territory through the scent glands on your paw pads. The second harks back to kittenhood, when you had to knead your mother's stomach to extract the milk as you suckled it from her; an act associated with comfort and satisfaction, carried through to later life.

The last theory originates from your wild ancestors, who would have pressed down and clawed at grass and foliage to create themselves a comfortable bed. I thought this was the most likely explanation for you. Partly because it correlated with your feral growl at mealtimes, but it also rang true because a good kneading session would often finish with you curling up on my belly and settling down for a snooze. This resolution made me happy for two reasons. Firstly, seeing you content and peaceful, lying on me, made my heart burst with a deep maternal affection. And secondly, my skin finally had some relief from the needling. Dean found an effective deterrent for this behaviour, by tensing his muscles. A solid surface wasn't conducive for your pummelling. Dean had a wash-board stomach that he could tighten at will, but when I tried this tactic, I still had a layer of soft flesh plenty deep enough for you to dig into. I'd grab a cushion or blanket to place in between us, carefully lifting you and attempting to slide it under you seamlessly, so you could continue digging with your claws without lacerating me at the same time. Sometimes it worked, but often you'd stop and move away, dissatisfied with the interruption and the inadequate alternative I'd presented.

As with all cats, or dogs for that matter, or indeed humans, your digestive system would occasionally need to expel some excess air. OKAY, yes, I'm talking about farting. Your farts were awful! They were always silent, but it was shocking that such a vile smell could emanate from such a delicate and beautiful body. Plus, I found it particularly insulting that you would just happen to pass gas when your bottom was within close proximity to my face. It usually occurred when you were lying on my chest facing my feet, or standing on my lap, with your hind end pointing towards me, as if locating its target. Undoubtedly you farted at other times, when you weren't near me, but it did feel like you saved them up especially, even though you didn't seem to notice you were doing it. I was lying in bed with you one evening when I needed to break wind. I got out from under the covers and manoeuvred myself so my rear end was close to your face, before letting it go. Like yours, it was quiet, but the smell had no effect on you whatsoever. My infantile attempt at revenge fell completely flat, and I was left giggling to myself like an idiot.

Your habit of sitting or lying on me was mutually beneficial, and it bonded us. I loved feeling your little heartbeat against my skin, your purr vibrating against my lap like a tiny engine, and the comforting glow of your body heat radiating through me. Your sleeping face was the perfect picture of serenity, and I felt privileged that you trusted me enough to relax completely – not just with me, but on me. In the summer months, you would move off when you got too warm, to lie somewhere cooler, but in the bitter winter of 2010 we kept each other snug and you were eager to settle down on me at any opportunity.

We were living in a house by then, back near Cromwell Road. It was lovely and homely, and you had a cat flap to the garden, but the heating didn't work properly. The landlady didn't much care, and I lacked the confidence to argue with her. Dean was out most evenings, either working or drinking until all hours, so we snuggled up with blankets and I wore extra layers to retain my body heat. The bedroom had old wooden sash windows, which let the icy air flow in. I bought draught-seals in the form of thin plastic sheets, designed to be shrink-wrapped to the window frames with a hair dryer. They helped to keep out the chill, but with the radiators failing, the house still didn't get warm. That was the first time it was cold enough for you to concede to having a light blanket laid over you. Your appreciation of the warmth out-weighed the discomfort of the extra layer against your fur.

The older you got, the more you took comfort from lying on me at night. I naturally sleep curled up on my side, in the foetal position, so I would often wake to find you balanced on the flat edge of my hip, determined to use me as furniture in whichever way you could. You weren't able to stay comfortable there though, since my pelvis is relatively narrow. You would perch there for as long as you could, and eventually I would indulge you by carefully rolling onto my back, allowing you to climb over to the wider surface of my torso. I found it hard to fall asleep lying supine, but you favoured the soft padding and curves provided by my stomach and chest, over the firmness of my back. I tried sleeping on my front, but for some reason you wouldn't settle on my lumbar curve, even though I thought it would be a perfect, Molly-sized resting spot. Instead, I allowed you your preferred choice of my front. I have a vivid memory of falling asleep with you on my chest; your bum on my abdomen and your head resting on my sternum. I looked down, straight into your contented face, conceding that your comfort would always win over mine. When I felt the urge to move onto my side, I resisted, and gently stroked your head. We woke in the morning in exactly the same position; you rousing just after me, realising it was breakfast time.

CHAPTER SIX:
Blindness and Vet's Visits

'I have lived with several Zen masters -- all of them cats.'

— *Eckhart Tolle, The Power of Now: A Guide to Spiritual Enlightenment*

Our new house on Portland Road was a short distance from Hythe Hill and back round the corner from Giles. A Victorian three-bed terrace, it was triple the size of the flat, had its own garden, and of course, stairs. So much to explore!

Around the same time, your vision completely diminished. That didn't hamper you, though, and you found strategies to assist with getting around and living your life as normal, with little disruption. When you crossed a threshold into a different room, you'd recognise it by the floor texture, and you relied more and more on your whiskers for navigation. The transition didn't come without its teething problems, though, and it took time for you to hone your new skills.

Making your way around the house, you'd come into contact with a wall or piece of furniture and immediately turn and head off in a new direction. It reminded me of a slow-motion version of one of those retro wind-up toys with a 'bump and go' action. You'd slalom down the hallway as if inebriated, touching one wall and then the other, zig-zagging along, until you came to the doorway to the living room, or the step down into the kitchen.

This method of finding your way about would take you on a scenic route to your destination. If your target was the sitting room, you would frequently end up on the wrong side of the hallway and sniffing around to find it. Sometimes you were aiming for the stairs, which required a walk to the front door and then doubling back round to the left. Being a lady of leisure, with all the time in the world, you bumbled along and reached your chosen location, eventually.

Your blindness felt cruelly ironic, given that your eyes resembled vast shiny globes on your modest face. Mottled iridescent shades of yellow-green, pierced with pupils that expanded and shape-shifted for no logical reason. Sometimes they were huge black circles, absorbing the irises from the inside out, at others they were long, narrow vertical slits. The variation was random and not, as expected, a direct response to light, which puzzled at least one vet we saw. Apparently this ruled out the possibility of a detached retina, or a condition that was otherwise curable.

The other odd trait you developed, linked to your loss of sight, was sleeping with your eyes open. I realised there was no need for you to close them, since they didn't seem to let much light in, anyway. That said, it was still unnerving to watch you dormant and dreaming while staring, wide-eyed, into space.

Moving house was not a challenge that daunted you, as you found your way around and settled in with ease. You learnt the new layout of our existing furniture and worked out heights of unfamiliar objects in no time at all. You would discover how tall something was by climbing up it, but wouldn't brave the descent unless you could get your front paw onto a solid surface below. However, your confidence quickly grew, and it was wonderful to see you jumping about, sometimes quite literally taking a leap of faith.

Dean came up with a rather mean game he liked to play with you. The scaling up of our accommodation had provided space for a larger cat tree. With three tiers, a den and a toy dangling at the bottom, it was a significant upgrade from the botched-up basic scratching post you were used to. The highest platform stood about a metre from the floor, with the next one roughly 40 centimetres below, offset by 90 degrees. They were spaced slightly too far apart for you to reach down to the lower level whilst holding your balance at the top, and the irregularity of the structure confused you. Dean would find it highly amusing to put you on the upper tier and watch as you attempted to get back down. You would pace around the small fur-covered square, occasionally crouching and stretching a paw from an edge, fishing for a surface below, unable to find a foothold. Your front leg wasn't quite long enough to touch the central post underneath, which would have given you the confidence and stability to lower yourself a little further and reach the next platform. I would only watch for a minute before giving you a helping hand, as I couldn't bear to see you struggle.

Another indication of your lack of sight was your reaction when spoken to. You wouldn't always respond when I called, but if your interest was piqued, you would turn your head roughly in my direction, your gaze floating somewhere in the middle-distance. Aiming your meow across the room, it was clear you weren't sure exactly where I was. My heart melted with sorrow, but at the same time I loved you all the more for your fragility.

I often wondered what it must have been like for you, coping with your blindness, and whether it made you sad. If it did, you hid it well, refusing to let your limitations hinder you.

In March of that year, you took to peeing outside your toilet again; on the carpet in the corner of the hallway. Out came all the measures I had tried the last time, starting with changing out your litter more frequently, and then experimenting with different types. Pellets, paper, clumping, non-clumping. I knew what your preference was, and also mine for ease of cleaning up, but we went through the cycle of variants just in case, and altered the amounts in the tray to see if that made a difference. It didn't. Next, I bought extra litter trays and placed them around the house, so you always had plenty of options for where to go. Your diet hadn't changed and nothing else about your behaviour was unusual, so I quickly grew concerned about what the underlying cause might be. This time I took you to the vet.

A blood test revealed you had early stages of kidney disease. The vet prescribed low protein food to assist your renal function. As soon as you started the new diet, you returned to your normal self, with an instant improvement in your toilet behaviour. The only difference then was having to buy expensive provisions from the vet, and cut back on your favourite fresh meat treats. I stopped sharing my meals with you, but I still occasionally gave you a bit of chicken or tuna. You loved it so much I decided that if it were to reduce your lifespan by a few hours, or days, it was probably worth the pleasure you took from it.

I felt mean withholding my sought-after leftovers. I filled your dish with the same brown/grey, bland-looking, shiny, lumpy mess day in and day out, whereas my diet was diverse and colourful. Having said that, I was grateful to discover that you rather liked the prescription food. When offered the regular shop brands, you were fussy, refusing to eat the gravy varieties for more than two meals in a row. It had to be the 'meat in jelly' options, and you would lick off all the said jelly before reluctantly chewing up the remaining processed chunks. The prescribed pouches only came in gravy, so you didn't get a choice, but thankfully you approved enough to consume it twice a day. The only non-fish flavour was chicken, so that was what you were stuck with. To my relief, you devoured it daily without getting bored. You also enjoyed the prescription dry food, which was another pleasant surprise, since you turned your nose up at most dried snacks and treats. There had only been one other brand of kibble you'd ever agreed to eat. I learned that most supermarket-stocked dry cat food is actually bad for feline health, even contributing to kidney disease in some cases. It's always worth asking your vet's advice on the best diet for your pet.

Another change we made to support your kidney health was swapping out your drinking bowl for a water fountain. The vet advised that cats drink so infrequently it can be a red flag if we notice them doing it; an indicator of excessive consumption that could signal disease. On the other hand, I also needed to ensure you were drinking enough. Cats are attracted to flowing water, like taps and drips, and natural pools and puddles: generally anywhere other than their designated dish. You were no different, making it hard to keep track of your daily fluid intake. The fountain provided an appealing and novel moving source, so you lapped from it frequently.

I've also since learnt that cats are unlikely to drink from water that's placed close to their food source. In the wild, cats hunt and eat their prey where they find it. Any very local water sources are likely to be contaminated with bacteria and urine from the animal it just caught, since the cat would be in its habitat. So, providing a water source at least a few feet away from the food dish may result in a more hydrated cat.

As much as you enjoyed the water fountain, there was one

other place you always loved to drink from: an abandoned glass of water. Alongside your poor eyesight, your sense of smell had also deteriorated. I often had to guide your face to your food, or you wouldn't know it was there. However, if there was a half-full tumbler on my bedside table - or any surface in the house - you would find it and drink from it, without exception. If you had a super-power, it would have been the ability to seek out a glass of water with no sensory assistance. Or maybe it was a sixth sense? Several years later, I lived with a cat who drank tea by dipping her paw into a deserted cup and licking it from her pads. Thankfully, she was clever enough to wait until it had gone cold first.

Only a month after your renal diagnosis, we were visiting the vet's again. The cyst on your back kept reappearing, and I became concerned. Despite having it drained, the abscess grew back bigger every time. At its largest, it filled my hand when cupped over your fur, and it wasn't unusual for the vet to drain away 10ml of liquid. I sometimes practised Reiki healing on you, which has been found to be very beneficial for animals, but you weren't comfortable with the direct heat it created, so I couldn't do it for long. Once in a while the lump would vanish. After initially thinking it had disappeared of its own accord, the second or third time it happened I noticed the surrounding fur was damp and matted. It turned out you had knocked it and split the skin, which was thinner and more fragile where the fluid had stretched it. So, I decided to get the cyst removed completely, before it really started to bother you, or in case it caused long-term damage, or became infected.

The procedure was simple, but it required an overnight stay at the vet's, which we'd never had to do before. As I handed you over into their care, I worried about how you would cope. You panicked if you didn't know where you were, and I was concerned about you being away from everything familiar to you, caged in and surrounded by strange smells and new people. I was overjoyed to collect you the following day and take you home to recover. A large patch of fur had been shaved from your back, revealing an inflamed wound held together by a dozen nylon stitches. It looked messy, sore and delicate.

The operation wasn't cheap, but I'd scrimped and saved enough money over the previous few months, thanks to my more stable income. I had debated whether or not to put you through the trauma, given that it was elective surgery for a non-life-threatening issue, but the cyst was only going to keep returning and potentially cause more serious problems. So I decided it would be a worthwhile investment in your health and wellbeing.

I had toyed with the idea of getting you insured over the years, but considering your age and medical history, it wasn't a viable option, at least not for a premium I could afford to pay. I sought some quotes from a few websites, but the standard questions on the forms weren't exactly relevant to your circumstances. For example, they asked if you had a microchip, which you didn't. I could understand that having one would reduce the quote for your average cat, who might roam for miles, take up residency with a neighbour, or even stray into a vehicle, with the owner driving off. However, you rarely went outside, and when you did you were hardly ever out of my sight, so it didn't seem fair to penalise you for not being chipped. There was no box to tick for 'blind and timid and therefore won't run away'. Or maybe that would have increased the price, as there was a higher risk of you getting lost if you did wander off. I came to the conclusion that it made sense to put some money aside every month for potential vet's fees, rather than fork out for expensive insurance.

After the operation you had to wear a cone over your head, to stop you biting at the stitches. These devices are also known as Elizabethan collars, due to their resemblance to 16th century ruffs. I don't think they were originally designed to prevent the wearer from biting themselves, although people didn't wash as often back then, so who knows? Anyway, you hated your plastic restraint. Considering how challenging life already was with your blindness, your new accessory only made everyday tasks more cumbersome.

An amusing outcome for Dean and I was that your trait of bumping into walls became even more entertaining. One of two things would happen: The cone would scrape along a wall as you walked close by it, keeping you in check with where you were. Or, you would arrive at a surface head-on, causing the cone to 'clop' as it hit, bringing you to a sudden stand at a dead end. If you were making your way to join me in the living room, I would hear your approach long before you got there, becoming aware of a slow crescendo of 'clop…clop…clop…' up the hallway. I would quietly go to watch you, my heart bursting with both pity and a guilty sense of schadenfreude.

The collar also made it tricky for you to walk up the stairs, with the bottom edge getting caught on the next step as you tried to ascend. You had to hold your head as high as you could while climbing up, and it would take you twice as long to reach the top.

Another task made significantly more challenging was eating. The depth of the cone stopped your face short of the food dish and your efforts resulted in a sticky mess scooped up into the bottom of the plastic, just beyond the reach of your tongue. I felt so sad for you (usually after some stifled laughter), and it seemed ridiculously impractical, so I took the risk of removing the collar for you to eat. The problem then was keeping an eye out for when you'd finished, so I could replace the cone before anything bad happened. After eating, you liked to have a wash, which was something else you couldn't do while restricted. Instead, you would meticulously lick the inside of the barrier. At least you were able to finish your meal, but it didn't help you get your fur clean. So, I would let you indulge in preening yourself, watching carefully as you did, and intervening as you worked your way towards the wound.

Once or twice, you started licking around the stitches, which irritated them. In turn, you would launch an attack and try to bite them off. I stopped you, attempting to balance tough love, to prevent a major incident, with kindness and empathy, knowing the frustration of an itch that badly needs scratching. I hated seeing you in so much discomfort, but there was little else I could do to help. The sutures looked delicate and the more you touched them, the looser they became. The wound didn't appear to be healing, but I told myself to have patience. Every time you were about to aggravate it, I would stop you, calm you down, and put the cone back on, hoping the stitches were still intact enough to be doing their job. As the days passed, your skin appeared to be knitting back together, and I felt easier about trusting you around it.

That weekend I was off work, so I went to Malvern to visit Dad, leaving you in Dean's care. While I was there, disaster struck. It was one week exactly since the operation. Your wound was itching, and you'd managed to slip your cone when Dean wasn't looking. Seizing the opportunity, you bit at the lesion, ripping the stitches and leaving the flesh gaping open. Dean broke the news to me over the phone. Being so far away, I felt completely helpless. He sent me a photo, and I rushed over to Dad's local vet for advice, hoping he might say it didn't look as bad as I thought. But it did. He said you needed to be stitched up again as soon as possible. I instructed Dean to take you back to the vet in Colchester and you were swept into surgery. Thankfully, they did a much more thorough job than the first time, using dissolvable stitches and polymer sutures. When I returned home the following day, the repair looked considerably neater, and within 72 hours it was healing nicely.

A few weeks later, with the sutures removed and your healed skin bearing new fur, you returned to your contented, happy self. No one else would ever notice that the tabby patch on your back had become more like a repaired quilt that no longer quite matched up.

I was constantly impressed with how well you cleaned yourself. Washing was a ritual you undertook frequently, and your gleaming white fur was always spotless and downy-soft. It occurred to me, as your eyesight got worse, that you had less and less reason to care what you looked like or how clean you were, yet it was rare to see anything spoiling your beautiful coat. This was probably helped by the fact that you moulted all year round. More so in the summer heat, but there was never a time that you didn't leave wispy white hairs behind you wherever you went.

CHAPTER SEVEN:
London, 2011

'I love cats because I enjoy my home; and little by little, they become its visible soul.'

— *Jean Cocteau*

In June 2011 we were on the move again, following a difficult and painful split with Dean. He and I had grown apart amidst work stress and a communication breakdown, and despite trying to patch things up, we came to accept it was over. Colchester is a small town, where you can't help but bump into everyone you know. We were bound to cross paths, the prospect of which appealed to me as much as the prospect of falling down a drain hole to avoid him.

The previous year I'd lost my job – the role I moved there for in the first place. Hopes of being settled for a while with some rare financial security unravelled, as I fell victim to staff cut-backs. To make things worse, as I worked my lengthy notice period, my colleagues closed ranks, treating me as if I'd already left. I became anxious and isolated. Not only was Dean emotionally unavailable, but he had chosen that same time to break away from his boss and go freelance. He was good at the technical aspects of his engineering trade, but lacked the people skills necessary to build up a client base. With no money coming in from his side, we were both under pressure to find work, and struggling under the stress.

Reluctant to head back out on the road while trying to fix my relationship, I took a job in a local call centre. The work was horrible. It's in my nature to help people where I can, but I was being paid to save the company money; looking for reasons for customers' motor breakdown policies to not cover their immediate problems. If we could bend the rules to avoid paying out - sometimes leaving people stranded with a broken car - that's what we were expected to do. All calls were overheard and recorded, and randomly selected for scrutiny by supervisors. If we said the wrong thing, or weren't deemed to be acting fully in the company's interests, we ran the risk of being reprimanded, or worse.

Family businesses are usually viewed as ethical, kind, and caring, given that the owners are building personal legacies to pass down through the generations. That one was the opposite. Run by a husband and wife team, with their son and daughter in management positions, the only impartial authority was the office manager. Not even she was deemed irreplaceable, though, and we all knew we trod a fine line between full-time employment and being let go with no notice or gardening leave.

I quit as soon as I could, moving on to an admin position for the council, in social services. My new role was much more rewarding, and my colleagues were wonderful, but in some ways it was just as frustrating as the call centre. Under-funding meant the demand from the community was stretched between too few staff. There weren't enough social workers, and it was normal for at least two to be off with long-term stress at any given time. Every day, I answered the phone to vulnerable service users and their families, forced to give the same answers to the same questions: 'Sorry, but you're still on the waiting list. We can't offer you support until you're allocated a named caseworker. No, I can't tell you when that's likely to be.' That list was extensive, despite each social worker looking after several clients at a time. One particularly compassionate colleague always had a large stack of case files on her desk, not wanting to leave anyone without help. It wasn't enough, though. When a client no longer needed support, their file was archived and the next highest priority case was allocated. Unsurprisingly, that was an all too rare occurrence.

The intensity of the work was alleviated by humour and friendly chatter. My colleagues and I would crack jokes and tell silly stories to lighten the atmosphere. Ours was possibly the only department in social services whose manager allowed us to indulge in banter through the day. Other offices worked in near silence, where general chat was banned outright. I didn't understand how those staff coped.

I had no ambitions to remain an admin assistant, or to climb up through the grades, which was a corporate concept completely alien to me. As a night owl, used to working unsociable hours, I wasn't cut out for the nine-to-five and I missed my creative calling. The final break-up with Dean was the catalyst I needed to make some significant changes in my life.

I met up with a good friend from my home town, who had lived in London for several years. Our friendship always remained strong, despite time and distance. Conversation flowed, and we put the world to rights, alongside sharing fond memories and a few glasses of prosecco.

'Hannah, I don't know what to do. There's nothing keeping me in Colchester, but I can't decide where to go next.'

'That's easy. Move to London. You know you want to.' She was right. Having grown up thirty miles from the glittering West End, in awe of the glamorous capital, I had always harboured ambitions to live there. Having been worried that rent costs would be prohibitively expensive, I decided I could make it work if I really wanted to. So, I applied for jobs and started looking for our new home.

Another friend of mine, who lived in East London, suggested calling her housemate Carl, to ask about viewing their vacant spare room. I arranged to visit, and made the one-hour train journey to Stratford. A bus took me east before a ten-minute walk to the address. The roads were busy and traffic-heavy.

There were a few essential shops, but no community vibe, or green spaces that I could see. The house was comfortable, but the bedroom on offer was smaller than I'd hoped. Despite the disappointment, I kept an open mind. If I could make it work, it would quickly resolve our house-hunt, plus we'd be living with a close friend, which would balance out the negatives.

After a brief tour of the communal areas, Carl invited me to take a seat in the lounge. Expecting a casual chat, I was taken aback as he started grilling me with interview questions. Put on the spot, I was rather nervous with my answers, but afterwards I felt fairly confident, especially as I came recommended by our mutual friend and housemate. However, I was acutely aware of a small furry elephant in the room, as you had been distinctly lacking from our conversations. When Carl asked if I had any questions, I grasped the opportunity to ask about feline practicalities, as you were the one factor I needed to ensure was catered for.

'As you know, I have a cat…'

'Urrr, no, I didn't know that. We can't have a cat in the house, I'm allergic!'

My friend had told me the housemates would all be happy for you to move in. I'd made the trip to London feeling hopeful about our potential new home, but instead I found myself back at the drawing board.

The following week, I secured a work contract with an opera company in Islington, but while my job situation was in hand, the task of finding somewhere to live didn't get any easier. As much as I loved the idea of us living in a place of our own, cost-wise it was out of the question. Even if I could afford it, a tiny studio flat wouldn't have sufficed. You needed space to explore and access to a garden, which narrowed down my search to a shared house. Whoever we lived with would need to care about you and appreciate your unique qualities.

You were getting on in years – about eleven at this point – although you didn't look it, being small and slim, weighing only four and a half pounds. While your average cat tends to be aloof and independent, you craved attention, so we needed understanding, feline-loving housemates. I was hoping to find somewhere with a few other tenants, to increase the likelihood of you having company when I worked odd hours. After a few trips to scope out potential houses, the best option turned out to be a flat in Finsbury Park, shared with just one other person: Paul, a chilled out, friendly young Northern Irish chap.

We had a large, airy bedroom with built-in sliding wardrobes and plenty of space for a double bed, chest of drawers, a desk, and my Papasan chair. The bathroom was small but adequate, and the open-plan kitchen-cum-living room was comfortable, and spacious enough to share without feeling crowded. Paul worked in the City and lived for the weekend, when he was often out at the pub. As we settled in, Paul and I struck a good balance of having ample time together at home to be sociable, but not so much to get under each other's feet.

Although you made many human friends over the years, you wouldn't give your trust and love freely to new people, they had to earn it. At first you were wary of Paul, but after a few months, when I was out, you resorted to sitting on his lap when it was the only one there. It probably helped that he also fed you when I wasn't around.

Since returning to single life, I was once again the only person you had a close bond with. You became my second shadow, trotting along behind me. Sometimes I would walk from one end of the flat to the other, saying, 'Molly, I'm only going to grab a drink, I'll be back in a minute.' But of course, you didn't understand, and you'd follow me to the kitchen, only to accompany me straight back to the bedroom. When I went to the bathroom, I would either let you in with me, which would feel a little odd if I was using the loo, or I'd shut you out in the hallway. Even if you hadn't initially followed me there, I would find you waiting patiently outside the door when I came out.

You often wouldn't eat when you were alone in the flat. I bought a timed dish, which I could set to open if I wasn't going to be home by your dinner time. When I got back late, you'd greet me at the door and then immediately head to your meal in the kitchen, clearly aware the food was already waiting for you.

You loved to sit on my lap at any given opportunity. It wasn't always convenient, but your cute face was hard to resist when my seat was the one place you wanted to be. Often it felt that your life goal was being the centre of my attention. If I was working at the dining table, you would make yourself comfortable on my paperwork, or on my laptop keyboard when I was trying to type. Basically, you would put yourself in the least helpful spot for me to get my work done.

If I was in bed reading and you were bored, or if I didn't wake up early enough for breakfast, you became impatient. In an effort to gain my attention, you would climb onto my bedside table, feel around for any random objects, and push them off. Anything placed there was in danger of ending up on the hard laminate floor. I would have to keep an eye out for breakables, or half-finished cups of tea at risk of your furtive paw. Despite your blindness, you played this game in just the same way any regular cat would; your facial expression challenging me to do what you wanted, or you would knock another item to the ground. The only way to stop you was to give in to that moment's demand, be it attention, food, or an outdoor stroll.

While living in the Finsbury Park flat, you took to spending nights on the sofa instead of in the bedroom with me. Every evening, without fail, you would pad into my room to check I was in bed, before disappearing off for the night. If I saw you in the doorway, I would talk to you, so you'd know I was there and didn't have to come over to make sure. Once I'd said goodnight you would head off down the hallway, returning at seven a.m. to wake me for breakfast.

At that stage in your life, you had all but completely lost your playful side. There was the occasional exception when I would dangle a toy in your face, brushing your nose and whiskers with it, to tease you. At first you would claw at the prey and try to catch it, but then quickly got bored and chose to wash yourself, or settle down for a nap instead. That said, I bought you a new toy that you immediately took to. Called a Kickeroo, it was essentially a tube of furry material, filled with stuffing and catnip, with a fluffy tail attached to one end. It was nearly as long as you, and wide enough for you to wrap all four legs around as you rolled about with it on the floor. That was you at your most aggressive, but you still looked more cute than vicious. You wrestled with it, inflicting pseudo-fatal wounds with your teeth and kicking the bottom end away with your back legs, while simultaneously gripping onto the top with your front paws, hugging it to you while pretending to fight it off.

Another toy you developed a liking for really surprised me: a small plastic ball with a bell inside. I don't know where it came from, but one day I walked into the living room to find you playing with it. As soon as you realised I was there, you stopped, but it thrilled me to see you re-discovering your kitten-like playful side. One-sided football became a secret game. You rarely indulged me by playing it while I was with you, or responding when I rolled the ball towards you, but sometimes from my bedroom, I could hear it jangling. Or I would catch you with it before you knew I was there, at which point you would walk away, looking completely uninterested. Occasionally, I would find the toy under the sofa, or in a different part of the room, which would give away the fact that you'd been kicking it around. You clearly loved your new game, but it was strictly a one-player, non-spectator sport.

Our flat was on the first floor of a large block, close to Finsbury Park station. Various retail outlets lined our section of Seven Sisters Road, including a Tesco Express, a bookies, and three fried chicken shops. We were at the back, on Rock Street, a pleasingly appropriate address for my taste in music. One neighbour lived above us and another adjacent, facing out onto Rock Street. Our apartment was inside the perimeter, our bedroom windows offering views over an expansive tarmacked roof terrace. On the far side, the flats looked out over Seven Sisters Road, towards the station.

Finsbury Park is a thriving area, with traffic, trains, and the underground all conjoining, plus pubs, restaurants, a bowling alley and various chicken shops attracting nightlife. By contrast, tucked away in our bolthole, we were isolated from the hubbub below, including parades of Arsenal fans that flowed past our block on match days. Secluded in our cosy pad, it was quite possible to forget that we lived in a very busy part of North London. During the riots of 2011, all hell broke loose a few miles up the road, in Tottenham, inspiring fresh mobs to start looting across the city. Paul and I watched the news unfold on tv with a sense of eerie surrealism that wild rebellion was unfolding just outside our bubble.

A patio door in the living room opened out to a small garden, sectioned off from the rest of the roof terrace. A neighbour's wall enclosed it on the left side and a thin wooden fence bordered the other two edges, with a gate leading out to the right. The ground was lined with gravel, and there was enough space for a plastic table and chairs. The one thing lacking for you was greenery. I considered growing some cat grass in a pot, but my fingers have always been more brown than green, with a tendency to kill off plants. I never got around to taking the risk.

I kept an eye on you when you ventured out to the terrace, but although large, it was sparse and open, so there wasn't much danger of you getting lost. In the middle stood an industrial air duct that blew out from Tesco underneath. It was surrounded by tall wooden hoarding, so there was no fear of you attempting to climb on it. The only risk arose when you jumped onto the small wall at one edge of the terrace, beyond which was a long drop to a street-level garden. Thankfully, you were never brave or stupid enough to attempt to descend from anywhere new that you couldn't touch the ground from sitting on. Also, you were instinctively aware of where your boundaries were, most of the time.

Having said that, there were two occasions on which you came close to running into trouble outside. The first was when you'd gone for a wander on your own, and several minutes later I heard you crying. I rushed out the patio door, through the garden and onto the terrace, but you were nowhere to be seen. I looked across to the other flats, but the roof was deserted. Dashing around the air duct, all I could see was empty tarmac. I called out your name, and returned to our garden. I could hear you, but your location was a mystery. Familiar but panicked scratchy meows seemed to be coming from somewhere high up, and behind me. Following the sound above my bedroom window, I spotted you, teetering in a gutter.

The roof of our flat also served as the garden for the penthouse above, whose footprint spanned both ours and our neighbour's apartments. A wide metal staircase gave them access to the shared terrace. You had climbed the steps, but instead of walking onto the secure footing of the patio above, you'd found your way along the edge of the building via the gutter. Realising your precarious predicament, you panicked and froze, before calling out for help. A fence surrounded the private roof garden, preventing me from simply walking up into it and collecting you, since we'd be on different sides of the barrier. I ascended three quarters of the stairs, until my head was at the same level as the plastic drain pipe, and called out to you. Feeling scared and stuck, you didn't want to move, but after a minute you started carefully edging towards me. I reached out as far as I could while keeping my balance on the step until you made it close enough for me to lift you down. Naturally, I was very relieved to get you back to safety without either of us falling to the ground.

The second time you went AWOL wasn't dangerous, but I may have lost you all the same. It was a warm summer's day, and you'd wandered onto the terrace. I'd left you to your own devices as I got on with some chores. When I looked to see where you were, I assumed you'd be sniffing around the walls or investigating beyond the air duct, but the terrace was empty. There was no splodge of white fur pottering about on the tarmac, or on the steps up to the neighbour's garden. My search became more urgent. I had only taken my eyes off you for a minute. How far could you have gone? Then I heard some excited chatter coming from the open window of a flat across the roof. One voice belonged to a young chap who saw me walking over and called out, 'We've found this adorable little cat wandering about – and it appears to be blind! I have no idea how it got up here!' You were perfectly happy and feasting on a bowl of tuna the kind neighbours had brought out, thinking you were a stray. They were dumbfounded by your appearance on the secluded roof terrace, 20 feet up in the air. I quickly solved their mystery by explaining that you lived with me, and pointing out our flat before thanking them, bundling you up, and taking you back home.

On a week off from work, I went to see my dad for a few days. When I returned, Paul informed me there'd been an invasion of mice in the kitchen. A few months earlier, we'd had to deal with cockroaches, and the pest control man was convinced they'd come up from Tesco. He'd looked me in the eye and said, 'If I lived around here, I'd never buy anything from that shop that wasn't well packaged.' On discovering the new furry visitors, Paul had bought some traps and subsequently created a macabre photo album on his mobile phone, of rodent victims in varying degrees of expiration. He offered to show me, but I firmly declined. I was glad to have been away during that particular episode. Not because I feared mice - far from it - but I wouldn't willingly kill any animal, except perhaps a cockroach or mosquito. Paul proudly regaled me with his tales of extermination and then told me you had been completely oblivious to the drama. At one point, he'd placed you in front of an activated trap. The mouse had other, more pressing concerns, and you didn't have a clue what was happening only a few inches away.

By this time, all of your senses had become dulled. Usually when one is lost, the others heighten in compensation, but this didn't seem to have been the case for you. When I put your food down, you wouldn't realise it was there. I would place you next to your bowl but you would stand there, oblivious, until I raised it up to your nose, or guided your head down towards the meal. Then you would happily start eating, as if it had only just appeared.

Your hearing had become selective too. There were times I would call you and you'd be completely unresponsive. However, the sound of a food pouch being opened, often as quietly as I could manage if I was setting your timed dish for the following day, would alert you from the other side of the flat. Loud noises weren't a problem. The hoover didn't bother you, and neither did fireworks nor any other intrusive sounds. I was spared the worry of you cowering in a corner if I was out on bonfire night, or if I needed to do DIY, or blow-dry my hair.

I mentioned in the previous chapter that you kept your fur immaculately clean. There was one exception to this, being the day Paul brought home some chicken wings coated in chilli sauce. I didn't think you'd like the taste of chilli, but you found a plate of leftovers and helped yourself. You weren't at all bothered by the flavour as you gobbled up the treat. I imagined you feeling delighted at your tasty discovery and thinking you'd got away with devouring it without me noticing. As you walked into the sitting room with an angelic look in your eyes, you clearly had no idea your entire face was stained bright orange. It was a good few days until that cleaned out, and you were probably mystified as to why I chuckled every time I saw you.

CHAPTER EIGHT: Special Needs Cat

'If man could be crossed with the cat it would improve the man, but it would deteriorate the cat.'

— Mark Twain

A year or so after being left completely blind, you developed a new habit of circular walking. You would pace in a roughly one-metre diameter spot, round and round, for several minutes at a time. At first I was concerned you were going senile, but actually it appeared to be your way of getting some exercise without bumping into anything. You'd find a space with no obstructions and create a little feline fitness yard. Usually, your circuit would slowly drift across the room until you came into contact with the edge of a chair or a wall. Then, using that as a guide, you continued pacing, touching the same marker on every lap, safe in the knowledge you wouldn't meet any obstacles head-on. The only video footage I have of you is from when my friend Sam came to visit, and using her as a central marker, you marched around her legs like a wind-up toy I'd let loose on the floor.

Sometimes you would meow while you walked, and I grew increasingly worried there was something wrong. You went into a trance-like state, like when pummelling my stomach, and nothing would break your focus. After a while, I'd gently talk to you, asking if you were okay. I tried stroking you, and interrupting your pace by setting you in a different direction, but you wouldn't have it. You were determined to reach your step goal, only resting when you felt you'd done enough.

This little quirk only added to my list of reasons for referring to you as 'my special needs cat', along with your scrawny meow, clicky hip, and complete co-dependance.

The Finsbury Park flat was our home for two years. It was a great place to be, and you were popular with friends and visitors, who knew you affectionately as Molly-Moo. At the end of our first year, Paul moved out to live with his best friend from Belfast, who was relocating to London. His friend's gain was our loss, and I didn't relish the task of finding a replacement. Living with Paul had been easy and fun, sharing household responsibilities, amenities, and even your care.

A girl called Lottie moved in to Paul's room. Out of the few people who had viewed the flat, she seemed the most suitable. Quiet but friendly, she talked about how much she loved cats, which of course was my top priority. However, it soon became clear that she wasn't as chilled out or as sociable as Paul. She kept to herself, spending most of her time in her bedroom, and the convivial communal atmosphere quickly dissolved, as she preferred to keep everything separate. Only ever using her own plastic plate, bowl, and cup, and her singular set of cutlery, she avoided the shared pots and pans, and divided up the fridge into 'her side' and 'my side'. Even the refrigerator door developed an invisible boundary line down the middle. Long gone was my prior ethos of sharing the milk, bought by whoever was passing the shop and checking in with the other for whether we needed any. If I wanted Lottie to put some food down for you because I was going to be home late, it felt more of a big ask than it had done with Paul. What was once a favour he wouldn't have thought twice about, with Lottie it felt more like I was asking her to move a small mountain for us.

By this time I was dating someone new, and I spent the odd night at his place in West London. However, if I left you for more than twenty-four hours, even with a flatmate for company, guilt would creep in for abandoning you. Despite it sounding like a pithy excuse: 'I have to go, I can't leave my cat on her own for too long,' I'd prioritise getting back to you. And you were always pleased to have me home.

An opera company I loved working with offered me a job on their autumn tour, which meant three months away. Every year it was the same schedule: Rehearsals took place in London, the show opened in Wales, and then performed up and down the country. Six of us would arrive at a venue at nine a.m., build the set, rig the lighting, and have a quick sound-check rehearsal in the afternoon once the cast had arrived. After the evening performance, we would take down the set, pack everything back into the lorry, and spend the night in local digs before driving to the next town to repeat the process. This intensive itinerary spanned twelve-weeks and didn't allow for much time off. I deliberated over what to do about your care for the duration. Broaching the topic with Lottie, I was hopeful she'd be willing to look after you. Although you were very low maintenance, it was a big ask, especially since she and I hadn't bonded as I'd hoped we might once she'd settled in. I didn't want her to take the decision lightly, but after considering it, she agreed. However, as the tour drew nearer, she changed her mind and said she couldn't commit to it after all.

Around the same time, my friend's boyfriend, Gary, was looking for some temporary accommodation in London, which neatly coincided with my tour dates. I didn't know him well, but he was friendly and keen to make a good impression. Sub-letting my room would get him out of a bind and be mutually beneficial, as he would cover my rent while I was out of town. Concerned that Lottie might not be open to the idea, I invited him round for dinner to meet her and see the flat. To my surprise, she had no objections, and after a friendly chat over risotto and wine, we all agreed to the room-swap.

With the arrangements made, I had a slight concern about how Gary and Lottie would gel, living together. Walking him back to the station that night, I tactfully explained about Lottie's quirks, stressing how unsociable she could be. Being an outgoing flirt and a sweet-talker, Gary wasn't worried. In fact, he was convinced that she was probably only introverted around me, and that he would be able to bring her out of her shell.

Gary was happy to look after you while he was there, which solved my cat-sitting problem, but although he worked in the City, I knew he didn't plan on being in the flat every weekend. I decided it was too great a responsibility to ask of him, especially as Lottie, by this point, wasn't willing to help at all. Also, it would have been too strange for you, having some random man occupying my bedroom. In hindsight, it was a wise decision, as Gary and I ended up falling out. He became nasty on the phone while I was away. He hadn't got on well with Lottie after all, and didn't want to pay the remaining rent money he owed me. Having snooped through all my belongings, he searched my computer for personal information to blackmail me with. His threats were baseless, and in the end he handed over the outstanding cash, but it was a very unpleasant situation.

Once the opera tour was over and we'd loaded the set into storage, I caught the train for the three-hour journey back to London. Emerging from Finsbury Park station, I pulled my heavy suitcase round to Rock Street and lugged it up the long flight of stairs to the flat. Tired and travel-worn, I was keen to get in, put the kettle on, and sit down with a rewarding cup of tea. I made a bee-line for the kitchen and reached for my trusty tea caddy. Opening the tin, eager for a comforting hot brew, I was horrified to find the caddy empty. All that remained was some pitiful evidence of what used to be there; a smattering of Assam dust settled at the bottom. Gary had sincerely promised me that any consumables he took he would replace, and I'd believed him, clearly foolish to trust his charming smooth-talk. Arriving home to a kitchen void of tea bags made me inexplicably angry. After calming down sufficiently to make a trip to Tesco, I opened the door to my bedroom to put my suitcase away. The room stank of weed, and I would later discover some more of my possessions were missing. The revelation of drug use went some way to explaining Gary's bizarre behaviour, but I was glad I hadn't trusted him with your care. Thankfully, Lottie had been detached enough to be unaffected by his theatrics. The only comment she made about it was that once he had worked through all of my tea bags, he had asked if she had any.

Instead of leaving you in the flat with two unreliable housemates, I had taken you to stay with my mum, Ros, who lives with my stepdad, Steve, in Farnham, in Surrey. They have no pets of their own, unlike my dad, and you had access to their large garden. You familiarised yourself with your new surroundings just as quickly as you had settled in anywhere else. To help you feel at home, we arrived a few days before my job began, giving you time to get used to being there before I disappeared. The house was also a B&B, and Mum didn't want you to make a habit of going upstairs, either into the guest bedrooms or her own. Steve had previously suffered with cat allergies, so they wanted to keep your fur away from the carpets. Downstairs had wooden floors throughout, which were easier to clean. However, within five minutes of arriving, you were up the stairs and sniffing around, confidently exploring.

I made up a bed for myself on the living room floor, to encourage you to accept that room as your safe space.

Consequently, it was where you ended up spending most of your time. On the Sunday, it was heart-wrenching to leave you, but I knew you were in the safest hands with Mum and Steve. I returned to Farnham at every opportunity. On a break from the tour, I visited, and before we travelled to the Isle of Wight, I stopped by. A particularly fond memory has stayed with me; that of returning to the house and heading straight to the living room to see you. Curled up peacefully on the sofa, I gently called your name to wake you. Your ears pricked up, and I said 'hello' again, confirming my presence. It was the best feeling in the world when you realised I was there, instantly recognising my voice. Meowing happily, you accepted my embrace, purring away in my arms. Leaving you to head back to work was horrible, but every time I went, I was closer to the end of my contract and being able to take you home.

Mum's B&B guests enjoyed your company in the dining room at breakfast, when you would go in to investigate the chatter. Initially, they worried about you bumping into the chairs and table, but they quickly realised you weren't fazed by it, as you simply changed direction and carried on. You continued to delight and amaze everyone who met you.

Impressed with how fast you'd settled in, Mum soon let you out into the garden to wander around and enjoy the sunshine. She was surprised by how adventurous you were, given that you couldn't see where you were going. One day, you disappeared through a boundary hedge to explore the neighbour's garden. Mum panicked, as she could hardly follow you into the bushes. She called out your name and heard a familiar raspy meow in response, from somewhere beyond. Continuing to call to you, she helped you locate her, until you got close enough for her to reach in and guide you back through. After that episode, Mum was grateful that you stayed within her boundaries for your outdoor exploring.

Most of your time in that house was occupied with sitting or sleeping on a favoured cushion on top of the sofa. At certain times of the day, the sun would shine through the window, directly onto that same spot, lighting up your sparkling white fur like a transcendent gift from the gods. I was convinced you were channelling Bastet, the Egyptian feline goddess, appropriately the daughter of Re, the sun god.

Around half way through your stay in Surrey, Mum became concerned about your behaviour. Your toilet habits changed again, and she felt that you weren't being your usual self. When I was able to visit on a couple of days off, we took you to the vet. Mum's cat Flora had sadly passed away the previous year, but she had used a local vet, Sarah, who she liked and trusted.

A few days before leaving for Farnham, we'd visited the vet in Finsbury Park. I wanted something to help calm you for the journey to Surrey, as the medicine you'd had for the drive from Malvern to Colchester had worked so well. After a full check-up, which I hadn't asked for (I wouldn't have minded, but it wasn't cheap), she recommended fresh blood tests to see how your kidneys were doing. She also expressed concern that your back teeth were rotting and explained that you would need to be put under sedation to have them cleaned, or possibly even removed. At the time I had no concerns about your behaviour, and therefore health, and I'd previously been told your teeth were in reasonable condition, although admittedly that had been some months before. Sceptical about how much you really needed any of the work, the quote of over £80 just for the initial tests made my decision for me. I'd spent the previous four weeks stock-piling your prescription food so Mum would have a full three-month supply, and that had taken up all the spare cash I had. I said we'd come back in November, after the tour, during which I could build up some savings.

Mum's vet Sarah was very thorough. With consent, she gave you a general check-over and asked lots of questions about your history. She looked at your eyes and enquired if you'd ever had your blood pressure taken, explaining that hypotension can cause temporary blindness and if that's the case, it's easily fixed. No vet had told me that before, or checked your blood pressure, to my knowledge. I explained what the vet in London had advised only a few weeks earlier, and Sarah responded that unless your health was noticeably deteriorating or changing, she didn't feel that further invasive tests would be of any benefit. She took you away to check your blood pressure and teeth. For a few minutes, I wondered whether, after all this time, your vision might be repairable. How miraculous it would be for you to be able to see again! But as I had suspected, hypotension wasn't to blame. Sarah confirmed that bits of your retina were floating around in the optical fluid, so your sight loss was permanent. As for your teeth, 'they don't need cleaning,' she said. 'I scraped off some tartar and they're looking fine – no rotting at all.'

I asked Sarah if she could give me more of the medication the previous vets had provided you with for travelling. Unable to recall what it was, I explained it had come in liquid form, in a small syringe, which I'd squirted into your mouth. She didn't know what that could have been. The only drug she thought it might be was a mild anaesthetic, but that wasn't something she would prescribe for a cat in your condition. Given your slightly irregular heartbeat, she deemed the risk too great. Equally, with any dental work, you would not only have to be sedated, but due to your heart issue, you would need constant monitoring. This, again, would be classed as high-risk and only to be considered if absolutely necessary. The last two vets who had seen you hadn't mentioned your heart murmur, which made me wonder how thoroughly they had read your notes.

Sarah said your change in behaviour may have been caused by my absence, and hopefully it would calm down again. Although the problem remained unresolved, the conversation had been very reassuring. The bill was cheaper than it would have been in London and worth every penny, given what she was able to tell me about you.

There was one other significant issue brought up at the vets that day. Your kidneys. When diagnosed, your condition was described to me as 'early onset of kidney problems' and that's what I'd called it thereafter, as your health had remained stable since being on the prescription diet. Sarah told me that cats with a deteriorating renal diagnosis rarely live for more than a year or two after discovery. That was a shock to hear. Either the vet in Colchester hadn't spelled that out, or I had blocked it from my memory. It had already been two-and-a-half years.

CHAPTER NINE: BACK IN LONDON, 2013

'There are two means of refuge from the misery of life — music and cats.'

— Albert Schweitzer

That November, I took you back home to London, glad to be there for you full-time again. Steve was relieved too, as not only were his allergies kicking in, but your circular walking habit made him feel quite dizzy. Re-settled into the flat in no time at all, you were perfectly happy to be in different, but familiar surroundings.

I had concerns about potentially needing to take you back to the vet, considering my trust for the local surgery, which seemed popular in the area, had been knocked. Other than another similar veterinary practice, the only alternative option I could find was the RSPCA, but their medical services were exclusively reserved for pet owners who are unemployed or on low incomes. Charities are vital for those on benefits, and the homeless, to have access to treatment for their pets. I would have loved to have supported them by paying full price for you to go there too. Given that they work on a non-profit basis, I would have trusted them to only prescribe medicines or recommend procedures if they were absolutely necessary. As it was, my options were limited to the pot-luck practices nearby. I just had to hope that you'd remain healthy for the time being.

In January 2013, I started a job in West London, in a private school that not only had its own purpose-built theatre, but employed two full-time members of staff to run it. I was the new Theatre Manager, working with the Technical Manager, alongside the drama department. My commute ran anywhere between thirty and ninety minutes, depending on the time of day, my chosen means of transport, and the regularity of the trains and tube services. The cheapest ticket option sent me on a convoluted route, incorporating multiple changes between underground and overground and back again, avoiding Zone One, which hiked up the price. This journey took three times as long as a single direct tube, but saved me half the fare, so although we were back living together, I was out for extended hours each day.

It was approaching two years since we'd moved into the flat, and a renewal of the tenancy contract was due. The agency notified us of a fairly substantial rent increase, and they weren't open to negotiation, so I decided it was time to move again. By relocating closer to work, my commute would be a great deal shorter. Hopeful I could find a room in a shared house for lower rent, I informed Lottie and the agency I was planning on moving out.

There were a couple of websites dedicated to spare rooms for let, and even refining my search to West London, the list was overwhelming. Hunting out those willing to accept pets, and looking past the cheap, grubby end of the spectrum, I was left with a few options to consider. One house-share in particular looked perfect for us, so I arranged a viewing and made my way across the city. There were four tenants there already, three of whom were female and seemed friendly and sociable. I took along two bottles of wine; one red and one white, and both from New Zealand, as I knew at least one housemate was Kiwi. The chap who lived there wasn't in that evening, but I spent over an hour chatting with the girls while we drank the Sauvignon Blanc. I told them all about you, and they were keen to welcome a cat. The house was lovely. Just the kind of place I was looking for. I left feeling positive we could make a comfortable new home for ourselves there. They still had a few more potential tenants booked in to view it, but I was reasonably confident we would be among the favourites. Several days went by before I heard the news. They'd decided to let the room to a man, to balance out the numbers. I was gutted. I was half-tempted to go round and demand back the second bottle of wine. I returned to my online search.

The hunt for our next home took me all over West London in the following weeks, visiting house after house, almost all of which turned out to be wholly inappropriate. Although I had high standards, I was willing to compromise. However, even with a decent budget, there weren't many landlords who allowed pets, and I saw some terrible rooms to rent. One was on a quiet, leafy street in a sprawling maze of an old estate. It was detached, with a new extension on the side. A weathered pile of bricks and rubble in the driveway hinted that the property was undergoing continuous work. The bedroom on offer was in the centre of the ground floor, and appeared to have been converted from a dining room. Furnished with a rickety double bed, a small cheap wardrobe, and a semi-collapsing chest of drawers, my enthusiasm quickly began a snowballing descent. The door that lead from the hallway was made up of glass panels, with no curtain for privacy. Another glass door on the other side linked to the kitchen/living space. As the landlord showed me around, he explained that the couch in the living area was often rented out to sofa-surfers, who would stay for a night or two. Without a lock on either of the transparent bedroom doors, and the added likelihood of a random nomad sleeping a few feet away, I decided it wasn't for us.

The next house turned out to be on a dual carriageway, which I only discovered on arrival. The weather was awful as I traipsed for fifteen minutes from the station in the cold and wet, inhaling exhaust fumes while trying to keep my umbrella from blowing inside-out. In shivering discomfort, and discouraged by the smoggy A40 only a few feet away, I clung onto the vision of the promising photos in the advert; a spacious room in a cosy house-share with one other professional. I was grateful to arrive, but when I did, my hopes for our future home dissolved with the pounding rain. Having expected the property to be on a side-road, I was dismayed to find it centre stage to the thunderous traffic and acrid air. My disappointment was compounded by the discovery that the bedroom on offer was situated at the front of the property. And the pollution was just as bad indoors as it was out, as the other tenant was clearly a smoker. The whole place stank of it. A quick tour revealed worn-out carpets, a deceptively small double bedroom, and a kitchen badly in need of upgrading. I wanted to leave, but I was undecided which was worse; remaining in the house or trekking back along the busy road in all the elements. Before I could get away, the agent asked if I was interested in taking the room. Normally too polite for my own good, but annoyed about my wasted time, I was unusually blunt. 'No, it's not for me.'

'Oh, really? Why not? Could you give me some feedback for the landlord?'

With no idea how to respond, I made some vague comments about the main road and the smell of cigarette smoke, although I was stunned she'd even needed to ask.

Another place I looked at was already home to several multi-national tenants who didn't know each other. I crossed paths with one who wasn't aware the ground floor room was empty, let alone that an agent was going to be letting themselves in to show people around. It was the kind of house where everyone kept their doors locked and lived separate lives, with no sense of community. The vacant room was right next to the kitchen, so the other residents would be walking past it several times a day. If I lived there, I'd have to keep the door shut, and probably locked. The agent opened it and said, 'You can keep your cat in here, yeah?' I felt like replying, 'She's not a hamster!'

The room was a good size, with French doors leading out to a private patio. In another, friendlier house it would have been perfect, but the environment there was too segregated. Having lived as a mostly indoor cat, you were used to being confined, to a certain extent, but being limited to one room all day would have been too much. You had to have freedom to roam, so it was important the house felt safe enough for me to leave the bedroom door ajar. Also, I was not prepared to sleep in the same space as your food and litter tray. That could have been acceptable if I'd found a decent, affordable bedsit with a garden, but that was about as likely as you getting a job and contributing towards the rent.

An ad for a room in a converted warehouse appealed to my inner bohemian. The building was spacious and airy, with sofas and comfy chairs in the middle, and an open kitchen at one end. Various rooms on the perimeter of the ground floor were utilised as paint-splattered studio spaces for live-in artists. The girl who showed me around was warm and bubbly, and others I met were equally friendly. And then I saw the bedroom: a concrete shoebox akin to a cell, with no windows and just a mattress on the floor. Since it was so small, the landlord was prepared to throw in a second room, next door. It was the same, but smaller, like a walk-in cupboard, with no shelves, hooks, or hanging rails. Feeling deflated, I reasoned that warehouse life wouldn't suit us, anyway. The atmosphere in the building felt so relaxed, I feared that friends of residents would come and go at all hours, allowing you to potentially roam onto the street, and leaving it impossible to control the security of our living space.

Finding our new home was certainly proving challenging, and my time was running out. With only one week left to move, I stumbled across a solution. A Gumtree ad offered a room in a lovely four-storey Victorian terrace in Shepherd's Bush. The landlady was a wonderfully eccentric woman in her fifties, who shared the house with her two twenty-something daughters. The family were upper-middle class, displaying an outward appearance of affluent Chelsea-dwellers, but with the reduced means of working class career-women. Fenella, the matriarch, was a widow, and stoney-broke. Later I discovered the property was rented from a charity.

We arranged a suitable time for me to 'totter round' for a viewing. At the front of the building, a dark and dusty, long-abandoned shop space faced out onto the street. Behind it was our new bedroom. It was smaller than our room in Rock Street, but quiet and comfortable, and overlooking the garden. It felt a great deal more homely than most of the other shared houses I'd seen. The only other room on the ground floor was a large bathroom, which would be for our sole use. Stairs led down to a storage cellar, dining room, kitchen, and patio doors. The two top floors housed another bathroom, a sitting room, and the family's three bedrooms.

Fenella struck me as an 'extremely busy' person; always in a rush to or from somewhere very important. I got the impression the daughters also weren't home much, but they were all affable and easy-going, and the atmosphere was warm and homely. Having spent the previous year living with Lottie, I'd grown used to taking care of all your needs on my own, so I decided we could manage without other housemates to feed you. Especially as we were now only a short distance from my workplace, significantly reducing my daily commute. Most importantly, it felt safe enough to leave the bedroom door open, for you to roam.

With little time to lose before the Rock Street tenancy ended, I was relieved to have finally found somewhere I could see us being settled and happy. So, not wanting the room to be snapped up by someone else, I told Fenella I'd take it.

'Okay, well, there's no rush, darling. You have a think about it and let me know.' She came across as very intense while simultaneously a little too laid back. I was mildly panicked that I still hadn't secured us a place to live after the following week.

'My current rental contract is up next Monday, so I'm keen to get something sorted out.'

'You're welcome to move in this Friday, I'll just need a deposit and a month's rent up front. There's no pressure, look around and drop me a message later in the week, if you still want it.' Whilst lounging on the sofa, distracted by a magazine, she waved a dismissive hand in the air, which I took as my cue to leave. She hadn't grasped my urgency, and I didn't want to come across as desperate, so I said my goodbyes and called her the next day to confirm our new tenancy.

'Wonderful darling. Looking forward!'

The drive to West London took around an hour. Having already down-sized my living space and pared down my belongings accordingly, one trip in a transit was all that was needed. My boyfriend, Joe, was driving, a colleague called Neil also came along to help, and you were in the travel box on my lap. While you were unsurprisingly vocal, I wasn't overly concerned about your stress levels. There was no question of sedating you this time. Thankfully, the journey was short enough to render that quandary moot.

As we progressed through the traffic, I noticed something strange about your cries. Your desperate calls came in triplicate: 'Meow-ow-owww!' and the more I listened, the more 'Meow-ow-owww!' sounded like 'Let-me-out!' My moving helpers heard it too, and we all found it hilarious. Hopefully, you weren't offended that your objections to being imprisoned in your carrier were met with incredulity and laughter.

As always, you grew used to the new house with impressive speed. Given that you were now around fourteen years old, I was expecting you to struggle a bit, but I needn't have worried. Our new bed was a beautiful metal four-poster, with a deep, comfy mattress. Added storage space underneath was a bonus, but the whole thing sat much higher off the ground than the modern, low-framed divan in Finsbury Park. I decided to create a makeshift step, to give you easier access. Before I had the chance, though, you were jumping on and off the bed as if you'd lived there forever.

Since we occupied the ground floor and used the facilities in the basement, I rarely had reason to visit the two storeys above. The living room was a comfortable socialising space, but the family were usually out, so I spent most of my time chilling out in the bedroom with you. You weren't inclined to use the living room either, but on occasion, when you were nowhere to be found downstairs, someone would discover you fast asleep on one of the daughter's beds on an upper floor.

When we first moved in, I placed all your accessories in our room, for you to find them easily. Over the following few weeks, I relocated your toilet to the bathroom and consumables to the kitchen. I put a spare litter tray in the bedroom, but you didn't use it. I taught you how to get downstairs to your food and water, and where the back door was. There was no cat flap, but that was fine, as I didn't want to risk you going outside unsupervised. You loved the garden, though. There was a stone patio large enough to explore, and then steps up to a lawn, where you got to enjoy grass again.

Grass made you happy; walking on it, lying on it, and rolling around in it. I had to keep a close eye on you, though, in case you ate any. A natural feline instinct compelled you to use the green fibrous strands to clear your throat of furballs. That meant eating it and then regurgitating. Only you usually wouldn't wait for the final phase of the process to complete before heading back indoors. More often than not, you would chew up some grass, then go inside and promptly vomit on the floor. Twice. I learned that the hard (read: gross) way. I would keep you outside until you threw up, and then, thinking it was safe to let you back in the house, you would vomit again, in the kitchen.

The garden was south facing, and we both enjoyed spending time out in the fresh air and sunshine. I would recline in the lounger while you wandered about, and when you'd done enough exploring, you would curl up on my lap or stomach while I lost myself in a book. When the temperature peaked, you became uncomfortable and chose to move somewhere cooler. You weren't a sunbather like me, but on milder sunny days we spent lots of quality time in each other's company outside.

A large fluffy black and white cat lived nearby, and would often sit on the low garden wall, watching you with interest.

Some days, it would jump down onto our lawn, intent on approaching you. I knew that catching a whiff of its scent would spook you and send you running indoors, so I attempted to shoo off the furry intruder without disturbing your peace. Cue scenes of me gesticulating wildly, while using stage whispers to persuade the cat to go away. It looked at me blankly without moving an inch, then eventually took the hint and sauntered off in its own time. I felt a bit mean, since the cat was doing nothing wrong. However, for the sake of your wellbeing, I thought it wise to deter it from your territory, in the hope that it would keep its distance.

One day, when returning from the shops and walking through the garden, from the gate to the house, the monochrome kitty was waiting on the wall. I tried to frighten it off, hissing at it as it prowled along the stone ledge. I then spotted our neighbour on her back step, a couple of gardens down, throwing me a confused but disparaging look for being irrationally spiteful to her pet. It was only a moment before she disappeared again, so I didn't get the chance to explain the logic behind my hostility. She must have thought I was some sort of crazy cat-botherer.

As with all my previous jobs, the new one involved working odd hours. While mostly there in school time, helping students prepare for productions, the theatre was often booked out in the evenings for events and performances that needed managing or supervising. Since moving from North London, my commute was a blissful ten-minute walk through a leafy park (or an eight-minute rush when I was running late). The safer-after-dark street route only added a few minutes to the journey time. This meant I got to spend longer with you in the mornings, and when I worked late, I could easily pop home to feed you on a break if I'd forgotten to set your timed dish.

Fenella and her daughters were all lovely and made us feel part of the family. However, we saw little of them, and when we did, they were usually getting ready to go out. More often than not, they were behind schedule, and one or other of them would be searching for house keys or a mobile phone they'd misplaced. I frequently felt like the calm in the centre of a whirlwind. Left on our own, you relied on me almost entirely for company and comfort. Whenever I was there, you wanted to be on my lap or in my arms. If I was standing in my room, you would pace around my feet or try to climb up my leg. There wasn't space for your circular walking in the bedroom, but you sometimes got your exercise in the bathroom or the garden. That said, you were in your twilight years, although I hadn't realised it, and your pace of life was gradually slowing down.

CHAPTER TEN:
The End

'What greater gift than the love of a cat.'

— Charles Dickens

There were many benefits to working in a private school. One was free school lunches (not bad quality either). Another was having the extra-long holidays off, and unlike the teachers, I had no marking to do, or planning for the following term. Summer break began in July and I had eight whole weeks of freedom.

Six months after moving to London, I'd landed some casual work at Hoxton Hall in the East End, on the Front of House team. What had started out as one-off a favour for a friend who was short-staffed quickly became a long-term ad hoc side gig. There was something really special about the shabby historic building. I could almost hear the ghosts in the walls. The atmosphere was reminiscent of an enchanting old museum, where every previous performance had left its print in the brick dust. A kind of magic had been infused in the auditorium by every performer who'd trodden the boards and every audience member who'd gripped the balcony rail in tension, empathy, or pure joy.

The pay was pitiful, but the work was rewarding. A rag tag team of unique and quirky characters, the casual staff suited the venue's equally casual fringe vibe. We hosted a wide range of events, from weddings to gigs, and community groups to top quality theatre. Many of my spare weekends were spent welcoming guests into that 150-year-old hall.

A week into the school holidays, I had a Saturday night shift in Hoxton. The venue was around an hour away on public transport and I got home before the dawn chorus on Sunday morning. I collapsed into bed, exhausted but looking forward to a day of relaxation. You curled up on my chest and we both fell fast asleep.

Like an alarm clock I couldn't turn off at weekends, you woke me at seven a.m. sharp for breakfast, unconcerned that I'd only slept for a few hours. I roused from my dream state with whiskers tickling my chin and a wet nose dabbing at my cheek. Bleary-eyed, I climbed out of bed, walked zombie-like down the stairs and emptied a packet of food into your dish, before heading straight back under the still-warm covers. I'd barely spoken to you, other than a groggy acknowledgment and a little stroke as you started eating. In need of more sleep, I drifted into a deep slumber.

A couple of hours later, I was roused by a noise. I prized my eyelids apart, expecting to see a blurry white form padding around the door into the bedroom, and was surprised to find you curled up by my legs. It seemed only minutes since I'd fed you, and I was unaware you'd come back up, let alone settled on the bed.

The mysterious noise repeated, and I realised it was coming from you. It was like no sound I'd ever heard you make before; a peculiar gargled growl. You were fast asleep, though, looking content and calm. Dragging myself to full consciousness, my confusion grew as the strange sound came again. I moved closer and noticed your mouth was slightly open. You appeared to be struggling to breathe. I reached out to stroke you, talking, and trying to wake you, thinking that if you altered position or got up, you might feel better and snap out of it. Your torso was pulsating; lungs working double-time. After a few seconds, you went into spasm and started fitting; your whole body convulsing before tensing up, juddering again, and then stiffening. You froze. Time stood still as I looked on, utterly helpless. And then, a long exhale. A slow, yielding sigh. Rapid breathing followed, your delicate frame heaving up and down, up and down. You took another couple of breaths and then went into spasm again. An exact repeat of the first time. It may have happened once more, I don't remember now, but then it stopped. Your body stopped. You let out one last quiet breath and all life left.

I think I knew what was happening as soon as I saw you on the bed that morning, and heard that awful noise, but I didn't want to believe it. The holidays were just beginning, and we were going to have the entire summer to enjoy together. I'd planned on making up for all the hours I had spent away from you in the previous months. I felt ashamed, because I'd recently had thoughts about how I was tied to the house because of you. I couldn't go away for more than twenty-four hours without guilt setting in for leaving you. There was no doubt that you were getting old and that one day, when you weren't around anymore, I'd be able to disappear on holiday and not have to worry about your care. And then I felt terrible for having had those thoughts. I hadn't meant that I wanted my freedom right then. I wasn't ready to let you go. It was too soon.

Over the previous nine years, I had become closer to you than anyone else. Boyfriends had come and gone, as had housemates. I'm not so close to any of my family or friends that I speak to them on a daily basis. You, on the other hand, you were always there. Yours was the first face I saw in the morning and the one I always bid goodnight. You were at home waiting for me every day, and greeted me back from work with pure love and affection. We shared meals, naps, walks, and games. You brought me so much joy and warmth, and I was always glad of your company. You were the one constant in my life, a beautiful light in my heart. Within seconds, that was snapped out, with no warning.

I tripped up the stairs, desperately calling out for Fenella, but the house was empty. Numb with shock and back in the bedroom, I felt poignantly alone. What should I do? What can I do? Mum. Call Mum. Picking up my phone, I scrolled through the contacts for her number. I always tried the landline before her mobile. Steve answered. I couldn't speak. I struggled to breathe. Air stuttered in and out of my lungs as tears poured down my face. Steve panicked, unsure of who it was or what was going on, until he finally heard me force out, 'Is Mum there?'. She came to the phone, told me to take deep breaths, and patiently waited while I gathered myself. The words I needed stuck in my throat. I didn't want to say them, I didn't want to make them real. 'It's Molly. She just died.' Saying it split my heart in two. Pain seared through me as my nightmare became reality.

After talking with Mum and feeling calmer, I went out to the garden for some fresh air. It was a perfect summer's morning, bright and warm, the kind I would normally relish getting up for, but the clouds in my head shrouded the day in a heavy grey filter. There was no one to hold or console me, and in your absence I felt lonely for the first time in years. I sat there in a trance for what seemed like hours, but was probably no more than thirty minutes. Eventually, I returned to my room, found a purple pashmina and laid it out beside you. Gently sliding my hands under your body, sorrow washed over me as I lifted your still warm, damp corpse, and placed it onto the soft fabric. It was the strangest sensation, supporting your weight with my fingers, feeling your clammy fur against my skin, your body limp and unresponsive. Unoccupied. Soma. I kept you in the same position you'd gone to sleep in, wanting to preserve you in your most peaceful and natural state. I didn't want to disturb you. You weren't there anymore, though. Free of your rickety, faulty form, all I was left with was a perfect, fur-coated shell.

I don't know what's on the other side, if there is one, but I guess we all have our own idea of 'heaven', whatever that might be. Maybe because it's too soul-destroying to think that a life could be snuffed out forever; a being, a personality, can just stop. Molly, I don't know where you are right now, but I hope you're having the most wonderful time. I hope your 50/50 vision is filled with beauty. I hope you can run around and play and eat as much chicken as you like! I hope I did right by you. I'm not perfect, but I did everything within my means to give you a good life and look after you as well as I could have. I'm pretty certain you felt happy and loved.

July 21st, 2013 fell in the middle of a hot summer. Being a Sunday, I had to wait until the following morning before the vets would open. On Mum's advice, I found a cardboard box to use as a temporary casket, although several hours went by before I gained the emotional strength to place you in it. When I'd wrapped you in the pashmina, it had somehow felt wrong to enshroud you completely, so I left a small gap in the fabric to avoid entirely covering your face. As I moved you, a couple of flies emerged from somewhere near your mouth. I desperately swatted them away, disgusted that your perfect body was being contaminated. I folded the material over your eyes and nose, closing the gap, and lifted you into the box. This time your remains were stiff. It wasn't unexpected, but that made it no less traumatic, so I did my best to detach myself from the reality of the situation. I closed the box over you, taped it up, and placed it on the floor before going to bed.

Sometime in the night I woke, worrying about the stifling heat. I took the box downstairs and put it on the cooler concrete floor in the basement. Returning to bed, I was bereft that you weren't in the room with me, but I reasoned it wasn't much worse than the stark knowledge that you'd passed away.

Early on the Monday, I searched online for the nearest vet and phoned them at nine a.m. Fighting through the tears, I explained what had happened and asked for advice on what to do next. The softly spoken woman on the end of the line offered her sympathies and said they could send you off to be cremated, and your ashes would be available for collection the following week. Through some additional research, I learned it was important to be wary of where to take your pet, post mortem. Many vets profit from using companies that collect deceased pets. They put them into bags, load them onto large vans alongside clinical waste, and handle everything the same way. They also mass cremate, and I didn't want to take the chance that they'd treat you like that, or worse still, make a mistake and I wouldn't get you back.

I asked the vet where the crematorium was and whether they deal with each animal individually. She reassured me all pets were treated with the utmost care and cremated on their own. However, she couldn't tell me which crem they used, and didn't have the information to hand, which made me a little uncomfortable. She said she would call me that afternoon with the details.

In the meantime, I researched possible alternatives and talked them over with Mum. I really didn't want to risk your body being carelessly thrown into a freezer in a bag, and then piled into a van with other animals dumped on top of you, only to have some anonymous ashes unceremoniously returned to my by a vet I had never seen before. My options seemed frustratingly limited. Then Mum suggested a pet crematorium in Hampshire called Dignity, that her vet had taken Flora to when she'd crossed the rainbow bridge. Tucked away in the countryside, hidden off a winding B-road, the family-run business pride themselves on an honest, personal and caring service, specialising in individual cremation. The idea of dealing directly with the crematorium appealed to me, and taking you to Dignity appeared to be the most respectful way to say goodbye. Mum drove to Shepherd's Bush to collect us and took us back to Farnham, before making our way to the appointment at the crem. The grounds were beautiful. Lush green lawns lined with bright, colourful flower beds, a garden of remembrance and woodland surrounding the Victorian brick kiln, all provided the most serene setting you could imagine for such a heart-wrenching experience.

Debbie - the owner's sister - greeted us on arrival and gently guided us through their procedures. She explained all the options and showed me the range of urns to choose from. I'd already looked online, and there was no question; your perfect final hiding nook was within a wooden cat, curled up asleep on a gilt-edged book. It suited you perfectly, since you loved to sleep on random things like magazines and newspapers, being cooler than the bedclothes or the sofa. One of my favourite photos is the one accompanying this chapter; capturing you using a book as a pillow, looking perfectly content. The publication of this story makes it even more apt. Plus, I like that, sat on my shelf, the urn resembles an attractive ornament rather than a macabre shrine.

Debbie offered to take a copy of your paw print. This was one of the extra keepsakes they had available, along with a fur clipping that was already included in the price. I wasn't sure if I particularly wanted your paw print, I couldn't think what I would do with it. A part of me considered it a bit naff, but on the other hand, I appreciated the level of empathy Dignity had for grieving pet owners, and how much a small tribute such as that might mean to some. 'Sure, why not?' I cast my self-judgement aside, figuring there was no harm in having another token to remember you by.

She then asked if I'd like to see you one last time, to say goodbye. The box you were in was still sealed, like an unopened gift, waiting poignantly on the table in the middle of the Farewell Room. I explained how I'd wrapped you up and that I was concerned about the high temperatures over the previous twenty-four hours. How the flies had been on your face and I was worried they may have laid eggs. The last thing I wanted was for you to be unwrapped with maggots wriggling out of your mouth, akin to a scene from a horror film. Debbie carried the box out of the room to check you over, and then brought you back through, curled up on a deep red velvet cushion. You were perfect. No evidence of flies, and she'd had to do minimal 'arranging', since you already looked so peaceful. I was grateful to have Mum there while I said my goodbyes. We both cried. It broke my heart that I would never see you again, but then, what was left wasn't you anymore. Your shell was empty and the light behind your eyes had gone.

Mum and I returned later that afternoon to collect your ashes. Fenella had suggested I could bury you in her garden, but I preferred the option of keeping you with me, as I knew I wouldn't live in that house forever. I plan on holding onto them until I find somewhere suitably beautiful to scatter them, or until the day you and I can be at rest together.

Soon after your cremation, an idea dawned on me. The paw print, which I'd been unsure about buying, provided the solution for something I'd been pondering for a while. I just hadn't had the right inspiration. Looking at the small framed image, I realised it was the perfect size for my plan, since your paws were as petite as the rest of you. After scouting for recommendations, I took the inky pawtrait*[3] to a tattoo artist on Frith street, and had it permanently etched onto my inner wrist. Now, I take you with me everywhere I go. In life, your paws had been very significant to me. Often, while you were sleeping or completely relaxed, you would lie with a leg stretched out. I would gently stroke it down to your velvet foot and carefully massage the tiny leathery pads. The significance of you allowing me to do that, without retracting your foot or extending your claws, wasn't lost on me. It was the ultimate sign of your trust. Now I have that symbol etched on me forever, as a reminder (as if I need it) of the love and friendship I will always cherish, between myself and my Soulcat.

---

[3] *Not a typo, just a pawful pun.

AFTERWORD

'Time spent with a cat is never wasted.'

— Colette

Dearest Molly-Moo,

You brightened my life the moment you entered it, and that same light was snuffed out the moment you left. You were a part of my identity, an irreplaceable piece of my jigsaw puzzle, my Soulcat.

I still think about you often and miss your company. My world has been eerily quiet without you. I miss the weight of your body on my chest as I lie in bed at night, and your wet nose and raspy meow breaking my sleep at seven a.m. I miss your warm, contented purr, your beautiful downy-soft fur, and your big, wide dysfunctional eyes. I long to once more feel you climbing up my chest and licking my chin to give me kisses, before settling back down on my lap.

There were occasions when my whole world was collapsing around me, but you were my one constant; my comfort and my reason to smile, providing me with strength, unconditional love, and pure joy. I felt guilty for not spending enough time with you, but I hoped you might understand that the long hours, and sometimes weeks, I was absent were spent working hard to put food in your bowl and litter in your tray. You were always my top priority. I made a promise to you every time I went away on tour that I would always come home and I would be there for you until your dying day, and in that respect I didn't let you down.

For the first few weeks after you left, I expected to see your furry face first thing every morning and again when I arrived home from work, and my heart would sink as I remembered you weren't there anymore.

I'm grateful for so many things. Firstly, that you came into my life all those years ago. I'm so proud to have been your carer, your mum and your best friend. I'm thankful for your unique temperament and your determined attitude in spite of your blindness. I was moved daily by your courage. I'm incredibly grateful you didn't, in the grand scheme of things, cost me too much money at the vet! Going peacefully at home meant no big medical bills, no drugs for old-age diseases and I was saved, not just of the cost, but of the trauma of a decision to have you put down when it all looked too bleak. Above all, though, I'm grateful I was with you in your final moments. I hope you knew I was there, and could feel me and hear me, and I hope it was comforting that you weren't alone. I'm grateful for knowing how you went. Even though I will never know what ultimately caused your death, I can't bear the thought of having come home to find you lifeless.

So, thank you, Molly, for everything you've given me, everything you've taught me, and for being my perfect companion for nine wonderful years of my life.

PART 2

The Real Tail

PAW-WORD

The following is Molly's story, told by her and translated into the written form by feline language experts.

Molly

('mɒlɪ) ~ noun. plural -lies

An adult female cat who is not pregnant or nursing kittens.

Queen

(Kwiːn) ~ Title noun. Plural -s

A female cat of breeding age, pregnant or nursing kittens. If a molly becomes pregnant she becomes a Queen.

PRRRRROLOGUE

'Trust is fragile, be mindful who you share it with' - Mummacat

When I first met Amy, I didn't know what to make of her. That morning, I'd just settled into my post-breakfast snooze when Jeanette called out to me. Normally when she said my name, it was followed by *'get off the couch'* or *'stop that'* or *'dinner!'* But I'd already eaten, and she wasn't telling me off. She sounded... nice. Then I saw the cat carrier and realised I'd been duped.

The dreaded carrier usually meant a trip to the vets, where I would spend several unpleasant minutes getting prodded, poked and stabbed. So I resisted being shoved into the plastic crate with all my strength and guile; fighting Jeanette and holding onto the edges of the door with my legs locked into position. Apparently Jeanette became wise, though. She lifted the top half of the crate clean off, placed me in the bottom, and put the lid back on before I had a moment to grasp what was happening.

Flashbacks of V visits flooded me with anxiety. The woman in the white coat would drag me out of the carrier by my scruff, onto a hard table I couldn't dig my claws into. She'd shine a torch into my eyes, stick a thermometer in a place I'd rather not talk about, and then come at me with the long, sharp, stabby thing. All the while, she'd be telling me everything was okay, which to my mind usually meant everything was really not okay at all, and was about to get worse.

Anyway, when we arrived at the carpark and Jeanette introduced me to Amy, she wasn't wearing a white coat. She was in jeans and a t-shirt. She had long, dark reddish curly hair, and was staring at me with inquisitive green-grey eyes. Or at least, she was trying to, as I hid at the back of my box, hoping she'd go away and I could go home again. She looked nothing like a V, but she had the same expression on her face; really smiley. The kind of really smiley I didn't trust.

Instead of being taken to a clinic, Jeanette lifted me into Amy's car. Then she handed over every one of my worldly belongings: The bed I pretended to sleep in until she went upstairs at night time. My toilet tray. The toys I played with on my own. My food. There were no other familiar smells outside the crate in Amy's car. The whole situation felt bewildering. Sure, I'd overheard Jeanette saying something about taking me away somewhere, but I had no idea what it meant. What was a Caravan, anyway?

1. KITTENHOOD

'Go out into the world my kit, and do great things.' - Mummacat

When I was really small, I was taken away from my mummacat and my brothers and sisters. There had been nine of us in total, all baying for Mumma's attention and climbing over her for milk. Most were tabbies like her, their whole coats flashed with light and dark brown stripes. She said it would help them hide in bushes and not be seen. I was different; mostly white, with a large patch of brown stripes on my back and down my tail. Mumma told me I had bits of brown on my head too, but I couldn't see those. She said if I hid in a bush, my white fur would stand out, so I'd be easy to spot. I'd never seen a bush before, so I didn't know what one looked like, but I hoped I'd never have to hide in one. My brothers and sisters and I played hide and seek every day, and I was always the first one found, even though I was the smallest. From a very early age, I knew I was not destined to win at games.

Mummacat taught us to eat for ourselves, from food hunted by the feeders, and she gave us lessons on how to cope out in the world. She was wise and experienced, and I absorbed her words as deeply as I suckled the milk from her belly.

When I was only twelve weeks old, my eldest sister disappeared. A feeder took her away, and she never came back. Then my other sisters were taken, and my brothers too, until there were only a few of us left. Different feeders came along and picked us off, one by one, never to return. Mummacat said we were each going to a new family, like the ones that brought our food. The same thing had happened to her when she was tiny. Every evening at sundown, she regaled us with the story. It was an incredible adventure of discovering new places, establishing territory and becoming the Queen of her household. My kitlings were very excited and made up fantastical stories about what their lives were going to be, each with their very own furrytail ending. I wasn't so confident, though. Being the youngest and smallest, I took comfort from Mummacat's company in our basket in the cage. It felt safe, and I wanted to stay there forever.

Mumma said she didn't know who our new families would be, but they'd provide us with shelter and hunt for us, and be there to fulfil all our needs. She taught us to cry out our demands so the feeders might understand, and she showed us how to use our feline charms if the mewing didn't work.

'While you're tiny', she said, 'feeders will find you adorable and lavish you with attention, but as you grow bigger, you'll need to charm them with your best features, and time your affections carefully to get the most from them.'

'What are my best features, Mumma?' I asked.

'Let me see.' She stood back, widened her dark eyes, and inspected me from nose to tail. 'You're lucky,' she said. 'your small frame will endear you to all species. Your face is round and fluffy despite your short fur, and your large eyes will serve you well. You'll be able to soften the hardest heart with those deep pools, my dear.'

I didn't know what I was meant to do with my deep pools and my round face, to soften the feeders' hearts. But Mummacat said 'You'll grow to understand.'

The thought of leaving Mummacat, my kitlings, and our familiar room made my fur tremble, and not in a good, purry way. I didn't feel ready to go.

'I can't look after you forever,' she said. 'I have other things I need to do. Besides, it's about time you learned to stand on your own four paws.' Mumma tried her best to reassure me, but neither her tough love nor her calming purrs soothed my fears. When the feeders came to take us away, I hid behind the others and cowered in a corner, or under the basket, to avoid being chosen. Eventually there was no avoiding it any more. My time came, and I was taken, too.

A giant hand slipped under my belly and scooped me up, lifting me high into the air. The way the fingers gripped me, I couldn't squirm away or make myself into a tiny ball, to hide. Looking down at Mummacat, I hoped she would shout out and tell the feeder to put me back where I belonged. Instead, she gazed up at me with a tear in her eye and a warm smile, and meowed that she was proud of me and that I was going to be fine.

A moment later, everything went black. The feeder had placed me into a cardboard box, with a lid closed over the top. I tried to investigate, but the space was small and cramped. There were holes in the lid where light shone through, but I couldn't see anything, just bright dots, shimmering like flecks of glitter. The box moved up and down and side to side and then stopped. A strange vibration coursed through the walls, and I struggled to keep my balance as the dark room shifted and tilted, sending me sliding from one side to the other. I had no idea what was happening. Was I to live in a tiny wobbling room forever? Would I ever be given food and water again? Would I perish and live out my last days in a dark cardboard prison, all alone? My mouth clagged up as a deep thirst set in, and it occurred to me I'd taken my last suckle of Mummacat's succulent milk. As I readied myself to cry out for help, the vibrations shaking through my box juddered to a halt. I heard a door open, and the floor shifted beneath my paws again, swinging to one side before raising up into the air. After a few minutes, it came to rest on a solid surface. A muffled voice outside said something I couldn't hear, and then a door clicked closed and everything went still.

The walls of my cardboard room smelled vaguely musty, but beyond that, a sharper, fresher scent spiked through. The aroma reminded me of a toy the feeders had hung above our toilet tray once. I longed to be back there, among my rowdy kitlings, tumbling and feuding and running around. Mumma would be in the basket, watching over us, keeping order and patiently gathering us up if we strayed too far. In the midst of my memories, a deafening scraping noise jolted me back to reality. The roof of my box opened up and light flooded in. Then, like a dark cloud, a grey shadow cast me back into the gloom. A large bowl sailed down from above and landed beside me, sloshing water over the side. I lapped at it with fervour, my cruel catnapper becoming my saviour in an instant. The drink wasn't as comforting as Mumma's milk, but it was refreshing all the same, and my dry tongue would have been grateful for a muddy puddle by then. Before I'd finished quenching my thirst, a huge hand appeared and dropped biscuits next to me; dozens of them, clattering to the ground. I ate until my belly was full and then washed, as Mummacat taught me to do after every meal.

As I set about cleaning behind my ears, the box turned dark again. The lid scraped back into place, and after a moment, even the light through the holes faded to black. I curled up and tried to sleep. Hours trickled by as I lay in the silent gloom. Perhaps I'd been right, and this was it; my new life was to be lived in a dank box, my feeder occasionally dropping in food and water to keep me alive. What would I do when I needed the toilet tray? Mumma was strict about where we were allowed to relieve ourselves. All her lessons on hygiene, and how to behave around feeders, would be wasted if life was going to be one long, dark, empty nothingness. Had Mumma lied to me about what my future would be? I felt deserted. A part of me had hoped I'd be taken to the same place my kitlings had gone, and we'd all be reunited. My new reality was worse than anything I could have imagined.

I must have drifted off at some point, because I woke to the sound of feeders outside my tiny prison. When I opened my eyes, there was light glinting through the holes again. Footsteps running around were soon followed by high-pitched voices, shouting and screaming, getting louder and closer. Bigger, deeper ones called for calm before announcing, 'We have a very special present for you this year. You need to take great care of it.' My room moved again. It swung into the air before being brought down to land on something hard. I gripped the soft cardboard floor with my claws, holding my balance while my heart beat wildly in my chest. The squealy cries called out in unison: 'What is it?' 'I want to open it!' and the deeper voices replied 'Be careful,' and 'Slowly now.' Moments later, I was blinded by bright light. The box roof was pulled opened, and I mewed in surprise and fright. The high-pitched squeals set off again, but this time they were even more piercing: 'A kitten! Is it a kitten, Mummy?' The now familiar giant hand wrapped around me and lifted me out of my cell, and a huge room swept into view.

There was a gigantic tree next to me. It was green, but also dripping with shiny red and gold ribbons. I realised it was the source of the sharp scent I could smell through the box, although the tree looked nothing like the cardboard toy I'd seen hanging above the toilet tray. Various feeders filled the room; big ones and mini versions, all smiling and clapping, staring at me and reaching out towards me. Pudgy, sticky fingers prodded my fur and grabbed at me, while the big feeder that held me pulled me away.

'I said be careful! You don't want to frighten her.' It was too late for that. I was petrified. The chubby, smiley-faced mini-feeders backed off, but then the one in charge put me down on the floor. No longer in the relative safety of the huge boney hand, I searched around for somewhere to hide. There was no-where to run to. Behind me was the spiky tree, which also had flashing lights and dazzling shiny ball toys hanging off it. Piles of brightly coloured boxes flanked each side, and in front of me, a barricade of feeders cooed and pawed in my direction, each one calling me towards them.

'You'll have to decide what to call her,' a big feeder said.

One of the mini ones, wearing a puffy pink dress, with blonde pigtails, stared at me with an alarming intensity.

'Hmmm, Snowy!' she said.

Another girl, who looked to be a smaller version of the first one, but in a gold dress, with a plastic crown on her head, was dancing around on the spot. She stopped abruptly and pointed a long, sparkly wand in my direction. I cowered back towards the tree.

'Princess Twinklestar!'

A bigger one with short fair hair, wearing red tartan pyjamas, scowled at the others. 'No way. They're girly names.'

'But she *is* a girl!' said the dancing mini-feeder.

'Okay then. Becky,' he suggested.

'Becky's not a cat's name!'

'Nor is Princess Twinklestar, that's stupid.'

'It's not stupid! You're stupid.'

'Children, children, no arguing,' boomed a deep, loud voice. 'You'll have to all agree. Becky and Princess Twinklestar are both out.'

'Snowy then!'

'No.'

'Fairydust.'

'No!'

'Biscuit.'

'Snuggles.'

'Fluffy!'

'Cookie!'

'Ooooo, Cookie's cute!'

'Emma, do you like Cookie?' asked a big feeder.

'Yeah, okay. It's like, second best to Princess Twinklestar.'

'Right, decision made. Cookie it is.'

Cookie? Wasn't that something feeders eat? Hardly an appropriate name for a cat. I realised I'd have to get used to it though, as that was what they'd decided and I needed to at least try to fit in with my new family, as raucous as they were.

Over the following days and weeks, I became accustomed to my surroundings and the mini-feeders. The big ones called them children, as well as Emma, Katie and Tom, and it turned out they were like feeder kittens, only far less cute. The big ones were called Mummy and Daddy.

Mummacat was right about them giving me lots of attention while I was small. They played with me and ruffled my fur whenever they saw me, and they brought their friends round to ruffle me, too. But as I grew bigger, the feline charms Mumma

had taught me weren't working as well as she'd promised. The longer I was there, the less affection they showed me.
When the summer came, I occupied myself, spending several hours a day out in the garden. When I was first shown the outside, I could barely believe my eyes. A door that looked the same as all the others opened out to a whole new world. Mummacat had talked about the outside before, but I wasn't convinced it was real, since she'd never been able to show us. I thought perhaps I'd dreamt up some of the stories Mumma had told, or that they'd been retellings of strange dreams she'd had.

The first day Feeder Mummy opened the back door, and I saw the green grass and the trees and the bushes and the blue, blue sky, I was almost dizzy with wonder and awe. Cool air filled my nose with fresh, clean oxygen, and the world glowed with a wonderful luminescence. The grass looked sharp and spiky, so I was reluctant to step onto it, in case it stabbed my paws. Then I saw a ladybird crawling up the edge of a blade and decided it can't be that dangerous after all. So I tentatively pawed at a patch by the path and the long, slender stems gave way, bending under my pads. The lawn was surprisingly pleasant to walk on, like a deep velvet cushion laid over the floor.

The outdoors soon became my favourite place. There was always an open window in the kitchen or dining room I found I could get in and out of, and I started spending every spare minute in the garden. After a while, I even investigated the front of the house, walking up and down the road and looking in the neighbours' windows. It was fascinating to see how other families lived, and whether or not they shared their homes with cats. Some houses had canines, which came as a very unpleasant revelation. The first time I saw one, I was so taken aback at the sight of the excitable, yappy thing bouncing on the arm of the sofa, I didn't even notice a silver tabby creeping up behind me.

'Dogs,' it said. 'Goodness knows what purpose they serve on this green earth. They make the feeders feel more intelligent, I believe. Idiots.' I nodded in agreement, out of politeness, and then ran all the way home.

The next day, the rain came. Great sheets of water fell from the sky, turning the whole world a dank shade of grey. I wasn't impressed. Feeders need water to get clean, but I had my own methods that didn't involve feeling like a drowned rat. I saw one of those once, on the garden pathway. It scared the fur off of me.

Anyway, when it was sunny and warm, the mini-feeders came home from school and went straight back out on their bikes, or to the park. In the warmest months, they had a summer holiday when they didn't have to go to school, so I had a bit more company. Although even then, the children still disappeared most days, and when they got home, they were too tired to play with me. The smallest, Emma, was my favourite. She was home more in the beginning, and loved to talk to me all day long. I picked up my first basic feeder language skills from her.

The following year, Emma went to school too, and Feeder Mummy started a new job, so I pottered around the house on my own. In the winter-time, the children played with me as if I was an old toy they had rediscovered, like a dusty game of Operation, brought down from the loft. I liked to chew up the little plastic pieces they left lying around, in the hope that it would render the game useless, leaving them to turn their attention back to me instead. It didn't work, and come the spring they had outdoor entertainment again, and I saw them even less.

2. CAT PRISON

'If in doubt, get out.' - Mummacat

Half way through my second summer with the family, they took me to a cattery. It was like a feline version of prison I'd seen in one of the programmes the adult feeders watched. Goodness knows why they wanted to sit around staring at a noisy picture box, when there was so much real-life nature to explore outside. But it's what they chose to spend their time doing, so who was I to judge? When the outdoors was cold, I'd curl up in my bed in the corner of the room and sneak a glance at the magic window they looked through so intently. As much as I sniffed at their choice of entertainment, I also found it strangely fascinating. The box that filled up with little feeders moving about and talking to the real-life feeders but unable to hear them confused my brain. When I was alone in the room, I tried communicating with them, but to no avail. A thick, solid screen that clinked under my claws protected them from falling out. Either the barrier blocked out the sound of my greetings, or they were just plain rude. I stalked around the box, expecting to find the animated scenes behind it, but there was nothing there; not even a doorway for access.

After the mini-feeders went to bed, Mummy and Daddy made the box come alive with pictures that weren't as bright or as fun as the ones in the daytime. They switched between different channels and programmes, which changed the backgrounds and the tiny feeders. One of their favourites was bad feeders in prison, and it looked horrific. So I couldn't understand it when they took me somewhere that was the just the same, but for cats. And they left me there for two whole weeks. I didn't know what I'd done to deserve incarcerating. Maybe it was the time they'd left a chicken out on the counter and I'd helped myself. What did they expect, though? I'm a natural born hunter. As soon as I arrived at the prison, my senses were confronted by a host of horrendous smells and sounds, and I would have given one of my back paws to be put into solitary confinement.

Ever since being mercilessly torn away from Mummacat, I became a dedicated loner. It was clear to me that cats are meant to live solitary lives, and I would never again rely on one of my own kind. I couldn't trust another feline alliance, so I stayed as far away from them as possible. The cattery, therefore, turned out to be my worst nightmare: a large room lined with cages, almost all of which were inhabited. The occupants ranged from pouffy Persians and stuck-up Siamese to more chilled-out, grounded moggies like me. A few were timid and quiet, but most whined and cried, and the resulting noise was a constant cacophony. When I was hungry, I had to shout out over the ruckus. Breakfast arrived late every day, and they didn't bring food at all unless we made it clear we were starving. I never found out where they hunted for our meals, but wherever it was, the pickings were clearly slim, as the meagre slops dished out looked far from appetising. Even so, I had to eat, and the gristly, tasteless morsels were just about edible in small mouthfuls. Coated in a thin, salty slime, they put me off gravy-covered food for a lifetime. I consumed as much as I could manage, to keep my strength up, in the hope that one day I'd be allowed to leave again.

Religion wasn't something Mummacat instilled in us as kittens, but in certain desperate circumstances, such as being locked up in prison, I prayed to the great goddess Bastet. Several other inmates addressed the deity day in, day out, frantically repeating pleading mantras, and I found myself following suit.

After a week in the cattery, the desperate shouting made me hoarse, and I relied on the others to keep up the mealtime protest. The newer ones had to learn from those of us who had been there for a while, but I was losing the ability to pass the message on. With a deepening weariness, I spent more and more of my sentence curled up at the back of my cage, nursing an increasingly sore throat. By the time my family eventually came to collect me, I scarcely had any voice left at all, and it never fully recovered, leaving me with a permanent husk.

Two weeks cooped up behind bars with barely edible food and

nothing to do amidst the constant yowling was enough to drive any cat to the brink of insanity. The screws let me out into a run for fifteen minutes a day, in a yard with a hard dirt floor. A few metres beyond the metal mesh fence lay a lawn of lush grass, but I wasn't allowed out there to touch it. I could only gaze longingly, imagining the soft, dewy turf beneath my paws and a bitter crunch between my teeth. Instead, I found the communal toilet tray and did my daily poo (which had virtually reduced to rabbit droppings due to how little I was eating). Then I'd walk around and check for any new holes in the fence I might have been able to fit through. The meat on my bones became leaner every day, although I fluffed up my fur to hide it, and I was confident I could squeeze into the smallest gap. But I never found one, and before I had a chance to finish my full sweep, or devise a plan for my escape, I was manhandled back into my cage in the room of the yowling cats.

There weren't many staff at the cattery, and the screws I did see were mostly curt and unfriendly. There was one exception, though; a girl I heard them call Chloe, who visited most days for an hour or so. Around mid-afternoon I'd watch the door, waiting for it to open, hoping to see her long blonde hair swish into the room, followed by her friendly face and gleaming blue eyes. When she appeared, her warm glow filled the room like a ray of golden sunshine come to brighten the dark corners of my cage. Her voice flowed like warm honey as she greeted us: 'Hello my lovely kitties, how are we all today?' Chloe's eyes glistened and her red lips curved into a broad smile as she looked around, checking who was new and who she recognised from her last visit. Then she approached each pen in turn and took us out to give us some of the attention we demanded. But with so many felines to fuss, she only had a few minutes to spend with each one. Some of the others lapped up her affections, relishing the skin-on-fur contact. Others preferred a chat, enjoying having someone there to make their demands to. Newer moggies tended to shy away, cowering in their cages, scared of being taken off to somewhere else they had no control over. Chloe would reach out a welcoming hand, let them sniff her fingers to gain their trust, offer some comforting words and then move onto the next cage.

Fergus, an old black and white puss, was a regular at the cattery, so Chloe knew him well. Larger and heavier than the rest, he occupied a double-sized cell on the ground floor row. Chloe let him out for a stroll around before lifting him up for a cuddle. It was the highlight of his day, and he'd look over at me, past her shoulder, with a smug grin on his face, like the mouse who'd got the cheese. All I could do was watch and be patient.

Waiting for Chloe to make her way around the room as she visited each cage was like hearing the crack of a can opening, smelling the tuna, and anticipating the delicious treat arriving on the floor when you haven't eaten for several hours. When she got to my pen, she opened the door, lifted me out, cradled me in her arms and wrapped me up in the affection I so badly craved. Doing my best to ignore the smells of all the cats she'd cuddled before me, I closed my eyes and nostrils and relished the moment, enjoying her warm hands holding me tight. She knew just how to scritch behind my ears and whisper comforting, sweet words as I nuzzled into her neck for those precious few moments.

My immediate neighbour was a particularly vocal tabby called, well, Tabby. Clearly, her feeders weren't all that imaginative. Anyway, she seemed to think she was entitled to my share of Chloe's fuss. The whole time Chloe held me, Tabby bayed for her attention. 'I'll be with you in a minute, Tabby. Wait your turn,' she would say. But Tabby wouldn't relent and Chloe always gave in, putting me back in my cage and switching her focus to the incessant yowler. I cried out that it was still my time, but with my voice losing its power, I became more invisible every day.

Behind my cell lay a wooden wall, within reaching distance, through the bars. Soon after I arrived, I noticed scratches on some of the planks and I gazed at the markings, wondering what purpose they served. Any mog could see there was no way to escape from the cage, even if they were able to claw out a tunnel beyond. A few days in, I worked it out, and then I felt compelled to make my own thin lines in the wood. On return from the exercise run each day, I clawed a fresh mark, charting the growing length of my sentence.

....

Eventually, my feeders came to rescue me, and I was overjoyed to be going home. I could forgive the lack of attention there, since being ignored and left in peace was far preferable to the prison racket. And at least I got to go outside whenever I wanted, and lie on the grass. But the cattery experience left me traumatised, and being back in the house was overwhelming. I had hoped the family might have missed me. I half expected them to shower me with cuddles and affection, as they had when I'd first arrived in their lives. The thought of them rubbing my fur and talking to me every day, like Chloe had, made me purr with delight, but they were so excited about their holiday and new toys, they barely noticed my return.

As the weather grew colder and wetter, I spent increasingly more time hiding under beds and in cupboards, feeling sorry for myself. Lying there in the dark, I imagined the mini-feeders coming looking for me, playing a game of hide and seek. I waited and waited, but they never came. Instead, they took me for granted, like the old armchair, whose covers they didn't bother washing any more, and whose cushions they'd given up plumping long ago.

The feeders had no idea what I'd gone through while they'd been away. They seemed to think I'd had a lovely time, as they clearly had. Sure, they gave me a little attention when they grew bored on a Sunday afternoon, but I was no longer their priority. Then, one evening, I heard mini-feeder Tom asking Daddy if he could get a dog! My ears pricked up so fast I almost pulled a muscle. I couldn't live with a canine in the house, it was out of the question. Everyone knows cats and dogs don't get on, and I didn't have the constitution for a noisy, flea-infested hound in my territory. The thought of the feeders playing with another pet and paying me even less mind than they already did sent me into a tailspin. I'd seen enough mongrels in the neighbourhood to know how differently they're treated from us felines. My family would take their new pet with them when they went to the park, or on holiday. Meanwhile, they'd leave me behind and forget to play with me even more than ever.

I sloped off to a cupboard, had a good wash, and decided I must find another family to live with. One without a dog, who appreciated a feline presence and properly respected a cat's status. One who would love me like mine had on that first day I'd arrived, with the glittery tree and the coloured boxes. I'd learned all about Christmas, and how it happened every year. When the second one came around, I panicked that another kitten would arrive to replace me. Thankfully, though, the boxes were filled with electronic games and dolls; no sign of a threat to my territory. Relieved as I was, I hoped the memories of the previous Christmas might rekindle the children's excitement for me. No such luck. They were more interested in their shiny new presents. When I'd arrived in their lives, I was a tiny kitten, and they'd frightened me. Now I was older and wiser, I knew I needed a family who wouldn't take me for granted: feeders who would meet my needs and show me affection, like Chloe in the cattery had.

3. FUREEDOM!

'You can do it kitten, I believe in you.' - Mummacat

The following morning, I set myself up with a substantial breakfast, licking my bowl clean before heading out to find my new forever home. I slipped through a hole in the side hedge, carefully stalked across the neighbour's garden, and found myself in a back alleyway that lead out to a road I'd never seen before. I padded the pavements, weaving in and out of gardens and peering in windows in search of a friendly house to settle in.

Most of the streets were already divided into occupied territories, so I had to hunt out unmarked pockets of no-man's-land. However, the available areas were vacant for good reason. One bordered a house with a growling security dog that sounded like Cerberus, Satan's gate-keeper. Mumma taught us about him in a lesson called Friend or Foe.

Another unscented space encompassed a tall tower. There was no garden attached, and just one door in and out. The building looked thoroughly unappealing; grey and weathered, with identical windows repeated on every floor, as high up as I could see. They were too far away for me to peek into, but the whole place felt uninviting. The entrance had glass panelling, beyond which stretched a bland beige hallway with big metal doors built into a wall. I got the impression that once you were in there, it wouldn't be easy to leave again. As I walked away, I glanced back at the windows. One of the middle ones framed a tortoiseshell cat, its eyes fixed out on the view. The poor thing had no way to get out. Perhaps they had a garden inside, and a loving family, and everything else a puss might desire. She didn't appear to be in distress. All the same, being shut away up in the sky like that held no appeal for me.

I kept walking, straying further and further from my old home, determined to find somewhere suitable to settle. Surely I wasn't asking for much? Simply what every feline deserves, in fact. I didn't need a large patch, just a garden with a clean house, and a feeder that understood the rules Mummacat had taught me all those years ago.

'Feeders think they're the superior race, but they are mistaken. They live under the delusion that they own us cats, but that's a common feeder fantasy we allow them to have. In reality, cats are the true dominant species and, if feeders have any sense, they submit to our demands. They go out every day and hunt for us while we roam free and rule the feline way. Always remember your weapons of manipulation: Eyes, nose, tongue and paws. Use them wisely and your feeders will obey you. If all else fails, or if they're attempting to display superiority by remaining upright on their feet, rub your body against their legs until they relent. If they don't serve you in the manner you deserve, leave them for pastures new.'

Much of Mumma's advice eluded me when I was tiny, but the words remained in my heart and made more sense as I grew up. Her voice echoed around my mind as I wandered the streets and kept me going on my quest to find a better home with more respectful feeders.

During a revitalising nap under a dense bush, I dreamt of Mummacat and her lessons. On waking up in the undergrowth and remembering where I was, my heart sank. Then the words Mumma had spoken in my dream became louder and clearer, giving me the motivation I needed to resume my mission.

As I emerged into a garden, a silver tabby chased me out, accusing me of trying to steal his food, which I wasn't, although then my tummy rumbled. I'd been roaming all day, and I had no experience of hunting for myself. Mumma had taught us some techniques using toy mice, but my kitlings were faster and stronger than me. She said they'd all make fine mousers one day, which would stand them in good stead if they found themselves in the countryside. When Mumma watched me practising, she told me not to worry because I had a prettier face than my kitlings, and my big eyes would always save me from hunger. She said I had puppy-dog eyes, which I took as an insult, but she reassured me it meant that feeders would give in to my demands more easily. Clearly, she never expected me to end up on the streets, fending for myself.

As I walked, the sky turned dark and the night creatures came out, defending their territories and scavenging for food. I followed some hedgehogs who were shuffling towards a small fence hole and chattering about getting a meal. The gap was too tight for me to squeeze through. Mummacat taught me, if my whiskers don't fit without catching, my body won't either and I'll risk getting stuck. However, a nearby gate sat low enough for me to jump over.

On the other side, at the bottom of a neat garden, lay a feast to my eyes and belly. A grand picnic of cat kibble and meaty chunks had been neatly laid out in saucers, with a big bowl of milk on the side. While the hogs scoffed the kibble, I lapped up the meat. The hoggies didn't seem to mind. They kept their spiky fur away from me, and I gratefully vowed to share out any mice I managed to hunt in the future. Aware it was unlikely I would be able to fulfil my promise, the thought was there all the same.

Once I'd eaten enough to fuel me for the night, I had a good wash and moved on through the gardens. Most of the homes had cats or dogs already in residence. I was beginning to think I might have to consider sharing my new home with another pet, despite my intense dislike of canines, and my deep-rooted mis-trust for other cats. Cautiously, I asked a couple of moggies if they knew of any families in need of a feline, but they were more interested in protecting their own territories than helping me find a new one. One of them - a large, brutish ginger tom - pounced at me with a loud screech and chased me up a wall. I wasn't used to climbing, it had never been my forté. Jumping yes, but scrambling up walls, definitely not. I had no choice, though. I needed to get away from the tom, who by this time had backed me into the corner of an alleyway. How I managed it I can't tell you, but the next moment I was at the top of the precipice, just beyond his reach. Once satisfied I'd left his patch, he skulked away into the shadows, and I let out an enormous sigh of relief.

I looked around and discovered I was surprisingly high off the ground, on a wall that surrounded a garden. Walking carefully along it, I searched for a way down, but there wasn't one that I could see. The surface under paw was rocky and uneven, with a narrow-edged gate built into one side. After surveying the full length of the ledge, I discovered it didn't step down to a lower level at either end, and the gate didn't offer a more viable descent. Built out from the rear side of a house, the stone structure surrounded a very unkempt garden with long grass and wild flowers. The building itself looked equally uncared-for and the whole place smelled long-abandoned, with a damp, mossy aroma rising from below. I spotted lights behind the curtains, though, so it was definitely occupied. With no scent of any other animals around, it dawned on me that it could be a potential new home. The location was far enough from my last family; I'd been roaming for ages and had no bearing on where I was anymore. If only I could get down and into the house, the occupants might be happy to let me explore and take up residence. It certainly had potential. For a minute, I allowed myself to daydream about spending my days rolling about on the wild lawn and chasing flies around the flowers. As I came around from my reverie, I faced the fact that there was no hope of a happy future unless I could get off the wall and back to ground level.

A flat rooftop extended out at the back of the house, but it was a long jump from the wall and I felt less than confident about clearing the distance. I was used to jumping up and down between furniture and soft floors, not leaping across large spaces onto hard, rough surfaces. It appeared to be my only option though, as the drop to the ground looked even further and scarier. Since I'd made it up onto the wall to begin with, I managed to convince myself I might be able to do this too. The ledge was narrow, allowing no space for a run-up. I'd have to launch myself from standing, fluffing out my tail to steer me in the right direction and help me sail across the still, silent air. There wasn't a soul around. Not a feeder to assist me down, or another animal to encourage me on. Even the leaves in the trees seemed to pause their rustling, waiting for me to act. I thought about what Mummacat would say if she could see me: 'You can do it, kitten, I believe in you.' I said it over and over. The words gave me the strength and courage I needed to make the leap.

I padded on the spot, preparing myself; my heart pounding like a drummer in a marching band. With my gaze fixed on the corner of the flat roof, I crouched down low, adjusting my hind quarters to ground my paws and set my direction. Then I pushed off with my rear legs, thrusting as hard as I could and springing off the wall. As I flew up into the air, I pinned my ears back for extra streamlining and stared hard at the approaching ledge. Time slowed down, feline-fashion, as I made the leap; the world around me holding its breath in freeze-frame anticipation of my landing.

The week before, the mini-feeders had got excited about a film they were watching, where someone called Neo was leaping around in slow motion in the picture box. I looked over to see what the fuss was about. A film called The Matrix was on. The hero was fighting off baddies, spinning around in the air at half-speed while the world stood still around him. Tom jumped off the sofa, trying to recreate the scene, like a copycat. I found it most curious, as the children thought it was spectacular, but it's what us cats do all the time.

My trajectory peaked around half way. Stretching out my front paws as far as they could reach, I held my tail out firm, rudder-like, behind me. My heartbeat shifted from my chest to my ears, and the sound of it split the silence that had deafened me moments earlier. The roof continued to rise up towards me., its edge still looking a fair distance away. I was losing height quickly though. Engaging my claws to their full extension, I prepared to grip the surface. But I was falling short of my target, which swung higher and faster than I'd calculated. I flexed my front paws upwards, trying to catch the corner, and the tip of my pad made contact with the concrete. Instinctively, I curled my claws around it, but it was too late. My body slammed against the brick wall and my paw slipped off the ledge. I fell down to the ground, landing on my hip with an agonising crack. Everything went black.

4. CATASTROPHE

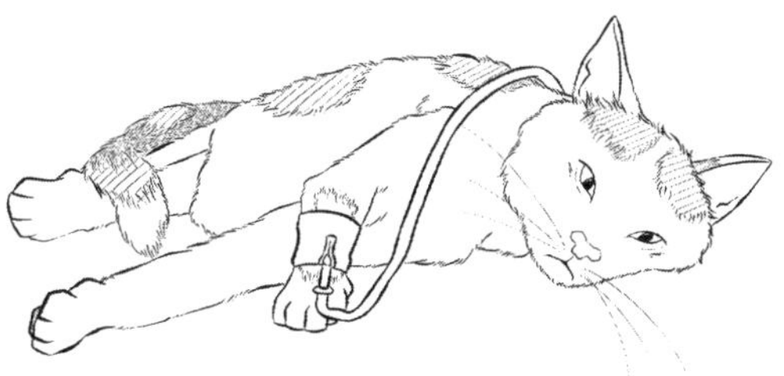

'Cats are capable of achieving great things. Whether or not they can be bothered is an entirely different matter.' - Mummacat

A deep, booming voice brought me round to consciousness.

'Hey kitty-cat! Are you okay?' Pulling my vision into focus, I was confronted by a tall stranger staring down at me with a wide-eyed and perplexed expression on his face. The owner of the garden I'd landed in, presumably. It wasn't exactly the greeting I had planned. As I drifted in and out, I heard the feeder make a panicked phone call. 'I've found a cat. It's injured. No, there's no collar. I don't know who it belongs to. I don't recognise it as any of the neighbours' cats. Sure, I'll bring it in.'

I tried to object, but the man wasn't listening. I didn't want him to take me 'in', wherever that was going to be, although I could hazard a guess. The only place I wanted him to take me 'in' was his house, to look after me and let me live there, and play in the garden. As I breathlessly stated my demands, he walked away, leaving me alone on the ground, unable to move. I felt completely hopeless; my mission had failed. As I lay there, lamenting my situation, he reappeared, carrying a blanket. He laid it on the floor and carefully lifted me onto it, wrapping me into the soft fabric, then gently gathering me up in his arms. The pain in my leg seared through me like a hot knife. But then it eased away again as he swaddled me, saying, 'There there, you'll be okay.' For a moment, I thought he'd changed his mind. He was going to carry me indoors, help me feel better and then accept me as his companion. His familiar. His mews!

He put me in a box, carried me to his car, and drove me to the V. Just the name of the place made me shudder.

The nurses rushed me through to one of the white rooms and shortly after that, I blacked out again.

When I woke up, I found myself in a cage, in a room worryingly similar to the cat prison. Convinced I was mid-nightmare, I scratched myself to check I was conscious. A sharp pain brought with it a flashback of my altercation with the wall. Not keen to dwell on my misfortune, I peered around the place.

The room was strangely quiet, since few of the other cages were occupied. There was a cleaner smell in the air, too - more chemical than animal. Definitely the V then, rather than a cattery. A very serious Siamese lay in the next pen, looking as worse for wear as I probably did. There was something stuck to his elbow, but I couldn't make out what it was. On checking myself over, I spotted a similar attachment on my front leg. Protruding from a bandage, a thin tube lead off to a bag of clear liquid. It didn't hurt. I couldn't even feel it, but I was concerned about what it meant. Was I being experimented on? I'd seen a programme in the picture box once, at my old home, about a feeder being turned into a fly. Could they be using me as a lab rat? Sleepiness overpowered me.

Some time later, a nurse roused me and asked how I was.

'If you drink some water, I can take the line out.' She rubbed my head and left me a bowl of food. After a surprisingly tasty and filling meal, I carried out a thorough wash and was relieved to find all my body parts still intact. The nurse said I was a very brave and lucky kitty. I don't know why. All cats are brave, I thought that was a given. Besides which, I didn't feel especially lucky, considering how I'd got hurt and that I was homeless and stuck in a cage in a V surgery. Feeders have this daft notion that felines have nine lives, like in a Super Mario game. I knew about that from watching Tom play it on his computer for several hours at the weekends. Cats aren't characters in computers, though, we're actual living creatures, and goodness knows why feeders think we can resurrect ourselves, like Jesus at Easter, with the chocolate eggs. Felines have many incredible qualities; some might say supernatural gifts. But I know from experience we can't cheat death.

'Who are your owners, sweetie? Where have you come from?' Despite objecting to the suggestion of being owned, I wanted to reply it was the man who had taken me in, although he must have already told them I wasn't his. 'We'll do our best to find them. In the meantime, you'll stay here with us until you're better. We don't even know what your name is! Let's see, I'll call you… Molly, I think it suits you.'

Not only had my great escape plan failed, I'd found myself stuck somewhere I really didn't want to be. The V wasn't as horrible as the cat prison, and the staff were much nicer than the screws (apart from Chloe), but I couldn't get outside or explore anywhere. My hip still hurt, albeit not as badly as when I'd first landed on the ground. The nurses regularly gave me drugs that made everything better for a while. Every day I got a bit stronger, and the pain eased a bit more. Eventually, I was taken to a small garden to walk about in. I was so happy to have grass beneath my paws again. I even managed to roll around a little, although only on my right side. If they'd put me in a caged run with a stone floor, like at the cat prison, I would have made some serious objections.

Despite feeling much better overall, my left hip jarred a little. It still worked, but not quite as well as before. The discomfort caused me to limp, and my bones clicked against each other as I walked. Weakness in my joints and muscles forced me to stop and rest at regular intervals, my rear leg periodically giving out from under me. Thankfully, as an experienced practitioner of Catha yoga, as all cats are, I was able to find a comfortable sitting position by stretching my rear leg out to the side in a Catalimbarasana pose.

Exercise helped, though, and gradually the stiffness and pain subsided. 'Keep moving, Molly,' said the nurse. 'We'll do a little every day and it will improve in no time.' She wasn't wrong.

Each morning, the staff told me they still hadn't found my owners. Something about my not having a chip, although I didn't eat chips, so that made no sense. The term 'owner' made no sense to me either. It's a word feeders use because they believe they rule us felines. Mummacat taught me better than that.

The nurses put up posters and leaflets, but no-one had come forward. They seemed to think that would make me sad, but it didn't. I had no desire to return to my old family. They probably hadn't even noticed I'd gone.

Everyone was calling me Molly by then. I liked it. Molly was a much more sensible name than Cookie. Not that I used it. Us felines don't need to label ourselves, it's only feeders that use identifying titles. Presumably because they all look the same, and they lack the acute sense of smell that we have. Anyway, I was happy to have a new feeder label. A fresh start was just what I needed. A brand new appreciative family to serve me and lavish me with affection. All I had to do was find them.

First off, I had to get out of the V. There were worse places I could have been, but there were also quieter ones. The other cats chattered and moaned all through the day and night. The more I recovered from my accident, the more impatient I got, and the less I was able to tolerate the company. I needed to leave, but I had no idea how.

Plan A was getting one of the nice nurses to take me home to live with them. Plan B was for the feeder who took me there in the first place to come back and rescue me, like Tarzan, swinging through the trees. I never saw him again, though, and none of the staff wanted me, even though they fussed around my cage every day, telling me how cute I was. As if I didn't already know.

One after another, I tried each of my feline powers, hoping to convince staff members to adopt me. None of my techniques worked. All the lessons Mummacat had taught me were going to waste, and my charms weren't having the desired effect. There was no Plan C. I felt like a big furry failure.

5. DOUG

'Every *feeder* is a cat person, some just don't know it yet.' - Mummacat

Once I was back to full health, a nurse told me they'd had to stop looking for my family. That came as a relief, since the longer they looked, the more likely they were to find them, and I really didn't want that. She said they'd put signs up in the waiting room, asking for someone to adopt me, and a nice man had come in and offered me a home. The nurse put me in a carrier and took me into one of the white rooms, where I was to meet him, and she left again. I was excited. Finally, a new home! No more living in a cage in a room with other cats. Then a thought occurred to me. What if this man already had a cat? Or a dog? What if he wasn't very nice and didn't respect my demands? My excitement gave way to nervousness as I worried over what the next stage of my life would look like. Would I be able to decline his offer? Or would I have no choice but to go with him and then resort to running away again if it didn't work out? The door opened, and the nurse came back in. Behind her was a tall feeder with dark hair and brown eyes.

'Doug, this is Molly. Molly, meet Doug.'

'Hello Molly!' he said. He had a soft voice and a friendly look about him. I couldn't remember how my last feeder had looked when he took me from my litter. I was too small and scared, and I'd been focussing on Mummacat as he carried me away. Doug gave off a trustworthy scent, and I was confident he and I should be able to rub along together.

'She looks sweet!' he said, as I flashed him my best puppy-dog eyes. 'My kids will love her.' What! No! Not more mini-feeders. I could manage living with just Doug, but not children, too. When kittens are old enough, they're sent out into the world to fend for themselves. Why do screaming mini-feeders have to destroy the peace and quiet of otherwise perfectly serene houses?

After chatting and filling in paperwork, Doug drove me to his house. In some ways it was similar to the one I'd left, but the scent of children wasn't so strong, and the whole place smelled altogether cleaner somehow.

'The kids won't be here until the weekend,' said Doug. Good news. Part-time mini-feeders I could probably cope with. In the meantime, I explored the house.

As I walked around, I realised the edges of the furniture were blurry - not sharp and solid, like I was used to. They went back to normal as I got closer, and they still felt the same when I touched or stepped on them. It must have been an optical illusion. I'd overheard my last family talking about those; when things look a certain way, but it's really a trick of the light. The light must have been strange in Doug's house.

There were three bedrooms and a bathroom upstairs. I quickly chose my favourite and scoped out some good hiding places for later. I tried out the beds and had a test-nap on the softest one. To do that, though, I had to make my first attempt at jumping since the accident. All the exercise I'd got at the V was walking around the little garden. The thought of leaping on and off furniture was scary, but making it all the way up the stairs with no problems boosted my confidence. The first bed I tested must have been for a mini-feeder, as it was close to the ground. I fixed my target, crouched into coiled-spring position and then pushed off with my hind legs. The next thing I knew, I was on the duvet and my hip wasn't hurting at all! I checked out the other rooms before curling up for a well-deserved snooze until dinner time.

A few days later, Doug's mini-feeders arrived. There were two of them, which was a little easier to deal with than the three in my last family, especially as they were only there at the weekends. Still, I was very wary of them and I knew not to trust their affections too easily after my previous experience. The new mini-feeders were called Ellie and Jack. They played with me and rubbed my fur and let me sleep on their beds with them. They ran around and created lots of noise, which was sometimes too much for me to cope with, so I'd go to one of my hiding places and take a nap. They made up for their disruption by bringing me gifts from the magical illuminating treasure chest in the kitchen they called a fridge. It's where feeders keep the hunting spoils. Once I'd taught Ellie and Jack what my favourite snacks were, they were more generous than Doug when they went in looking for treats. So all in all, they were bearable for the time they were there, and on the Sunday they'd be off again and the house would return to calm and peace, just me and Doug.

After I'd been there for a few weeks, Doug showed me the garden. It was large and green, with lush grass, a straight stone path, and a big wooden shed. Everything had the same blurry edges as indoors, but I had grown used to things looking funny from a distance. Most days, Doug left the back door open so I could explore at my leisure.

Doug was alright as far as feeder allies go, although he wasn't the affectionate type. I had the impression that he'd never had a feline alliance before. He fed me on time and petted me occasionally, but he mostly left me to my own devices, expecting me to entertain myself. I had to help him understand there was more to a cat-kinship than that. So, I pulled out all my feline charms. I tried rubbing up against his legs, but he moved away. Next, I waited until his hands were within reach and then rubbed my face against his fingers, nuzzling into his palms, so he was forced to stroke me. Gradually he relented and started petting me a little more often; patting me on the head or stroking my back. I rewarded him with warm purrs and padding for positive reinforcement. After a few months, he came to accept the fact that I needed lap time. It was essential for me to nap on my feeder at least three times a week. I used the body heat to recharge my energy as I slept, ready for my next big adventure.

Recharging was something I discovered when I lived with my previous family, way back in the early days when they appreciated my company. However, towards the end of my stay with them, they began denying me the right to lap time. It was one of the main reasons I had to leave. While I was between homes, and at the V's halfway house, I had suffered greatly from feeder lap-heat deprivation.

The recharging process took Doug a while to get used to. At first, when I jumped up on his legs, he stiffened and tensed his muscles, and then carefully moved me away, as if he was worried about what was going to happen. But we practised every day, and perseverance paid off. Once Doug allowed himself to relax under me, he realised how comforting having a lap cat could be, and we'd spend our evenings together, me snoozing and him staring at the picture box.

I learned a lot from the programmes he watched. In between my naps, I paid close attention to the words, and my feeder language skills developed further. I grew to understand the feeder sense of humour, which unsurprisingly eludes most felines. We have an altogether more sophisticated taste in entertainment. There were lots of different accents to understand, which us cats don't concern ourselves with in our language. We keep communication plain and simple to avoid any misunderstandings. Few of the voices from the picture box sounded like the feeders I'd encountered so far, but the words started to make sense the more I listened to them. I learned that feeders love drama, which is a type of programme, but also a way of behaving. Some cats indulge in drama when they're fighting over territory, but I can't be doing with that kind of stress. The drama Doug watched was all shouting and arguments. 'You're not my Mum!' 'Yes I am!' Honestly, how does anyone lose track of which litter they're from?

Doug laughed at feeders doing stupid things, and animals going about their business. He thought the animals were the stupid ones, but they were out there surviving without the need for picture box entertainment and manufactured lifestyles. Of course, cats are the cleverest. We leave the home-making to the feeders, then move in and demand they provide for us. You can't deny it works.

Once, we watched a film that featured a character called Catwoman. Needless to say, the whole thing was very silly, but at least feeders were acknowledging the true power and genius of the feline form.

Doug let me curl up on his lap during his evening's entertainment, but he didn't like me sitting on the sofa itself. He said something about me scratching the cushions - as if I'd be so disrespectful! Every time I jumped up, he put me back on the floor and told me to go and lie on my bed. Goodness knows why he thought that would work out. I was an independently minded cat, not an obedient, brainwashed puppy. So we played a game, in which I trained him to understand that I would nap wherever I wished. Each time, it began with me jumping onto the sofa and Doug moving me off again. Sometimes he'd put me on the floor, other times on my bed. Occasionally, he took me outside, but I'd just stroll back in through the cat flap.

To be fair, I didn't mind being outside, so sometimes I made the most of the free trip. I loved the fresh air in my nose and the grass under my paws. Grass is useful stuff. Regular grooming resulted in a build-up of fur in the throat, and grass helped me to clear it out. I'd chew on a few pieces until my mouth became wet and frothy, then the saliva mixed up with the fur and I could cough everything up together. It usually took a while for the whole process to take place. So, when Doug took me outside, I'd have a wander around and find some long tufts to chew on. Afterwards, I would trot back indoors and cough it all up on the carpet. He said my name a lot when I did that, and then he'd wipe it up with a cloth. Molly, Molly, Molly. I liked him saying my name. It made me feel important.

When Doug and the mini-feeders disappeared off to bed at night, they shut the doors so I couldn't go into the rooms with them. They wanted me to sleep on my bed on the living room floor, but I usually curled up on the sofa or the armchair, since they weren't there to push me off.

Then Jeanette came to live with us. She'd been in the house a few times before and she seemed pleasant enough, but she was even less cat-social than Doug. However, I'd taught him to be feline-friendly, so I was sure I could do the same with her.

Jeanette was allowed on the sofa, which I thought was very unfair. I'd sit on Doug's lap when it was just him and me, but Jeanette wouldn't let me on hers, even though it looked comfier.

They relaxed together on the soft cushions and I'd have to stay on the floor, or I would go and nap in one of the bedrooms, if someone had left a door open.

Usually, someone came along and kicked me out after a while, unless I hid myself away in a wardrobe or under a bed. However, I learned a hard lesson that if they didn't know I was there, I ran the risk of getting shut in. That happened once, shortly before the mini-feeders went away one Sunday afternoon. I'd gone under Jack's bed in pursuit of a snack he'd left hidden among the dirty clothes and abandoned toys. It turned out to be a rather unappetising morsel, but since I was there, I curled up for a snooze. I woke up to the sound of the bedroom door closing, and footsteps disappearing off down the stairs. Pressing my ear up against the door, I could hear the feeders talking. Ellie said 'Where's Molly? I want to say goodbye.' The others said they didn't know. I cried out from inside Jack's room, but they couldn't hear me. Doug said, 'We're going to be late for your mum, you'll see Molly on Friday.' And then the front door closed. Silence. I was stuck in that room for the rest of the day, and overnight. It was only the following evening, when Doug searched the house for me, that he eventually opened Jack's door and let me out. I was starving, and desperate for the toilet tray. Never again did I hide away in Jack or Ellie's bedrooms, for fear of being stuck in there forever.

I saw less and less of the mini-feeders over the next year or so. Especially in the summer, when they were out most of the time and I was left on my own, like in the week, when Doug abandoned me for hours every day. Apparently the place he chose to go to instead of being at home with me was called Work. I got quite lonely, as Doug's hours at Work seemed to get longer and longer. And then, when he was in, Jeanette was there too, taking up his attention. The children got bigger and spent more time shut in their rooms, or going out later in the evenings. They became too busy to play with me, apparently having more important things to spend their time on. I found that I missed the silly children's programmes in the picture box, blaring out songs and making them all laugh and play. The house had become so quiet.

6. HOLIDAY

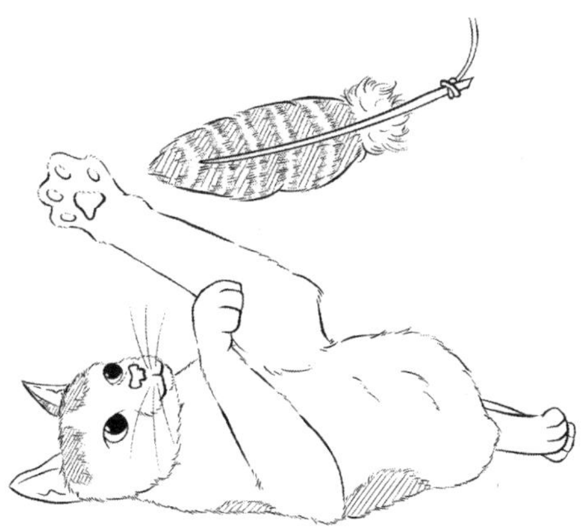

'I am Catwoman, *hear me roar!*' - Catwoman

Doug and Jeanette started talking about going away on holiday, like my last family had done. Traumatic memories of the cat prison came flooding back. My fur stood on end, my tail flicked, and I dashed upstairs into a bedroom to hide.

A few days later, I heard the word 'Caravan' being bandied about, which was a new one on me. Apparently, the family planned on taking me away on their break. I wasn't convinced, although I figured it had to be better than the prison. Then Jeanette told Doug she'd found somewhere else for me to stay, so I wouldn't be going with them after all. When she lured me into the carrier and lifted me into her car without Doug or the mini-feeders, I thought she was catnapping me and returning me to the V. Jeanette had never really taken to me, and in that moment it felt as though she'd spotted her opportunity to get rid of me once and for all. I didn't trust her one bit.

That was when she put me into Amy's car and I ended up at not-the-V-after-all.

Once the car had stopped, Amy carried me into a building, up some stairs and through a door. From the outside, it looked similar to the tower I'd walked past when I'd been looking for my new home, only much smaller. Anxious that I might not get out again, I kept telling myself the visit was only temporary. Another voice greeted me, different from Amy's. A man's. He said, 'Hello Molly! Welcome! I'm Craig.' Craig sounded a bit like Doug. A big face appeared in front of the box, but I turned around and hid at the back so he couldn't see me.

When the carrier stopped moving and Craig opened the grill door, I knew I definitely wasn't at the V. There were no white walls or chemical fumes. Instead, a carpet covered the floor, and the place smelled of feeders, although not like Doug and Jeanette and the mini ones. Crouching in the corner of the box, my nerves flittered between fear and excitement. Although I enjoy exploring new places, the uncertainty of why I was there felt unnerving. Craig and Amy kept saying my name, but I didn't trust them.

The carrier wasn't comfortable. The floor was a hard plastic shell lined with newspaper, basically a covered toilet tray, with no litter in it. Outside looked far more interesting, and I was keen to investigate, but I had no idea what I might find beyond the box. What strange new world had I been brought into? Amy and Craig moved out of my sight-line, so I took the opportunity to creep into the room. Everything was even more fuzzy around the edges than in Doug's house. I sniffed about cautiously, learning the layout. There was a sofa and an armchair, similar to the ones in my previous houses, and some other wooden furniture, and a picture box on a table.

The feeders were standing a few tails away. Amy reached out, tempting me over for a closer sniff. From where I stood, she smelled trustworthy, but I was reserving judgement, so I kept my distance and they let me continue my explorations. When I did eventually allow them to touch me, they were very gentle, lightly rubbing my fur: there was no prodding or pulling my ears back, or trying to look at my teeth. Once I had orientated myself in the living room, they showed me the bathroom, where they'd put my toilet tray. That's when I realised I wasn't on a flying visit. Earlier, Amy had said 'You'll be staying here with us for a while.' But I'd learned to be cautious with information feeders gave me, as what they say isn't always what they mean, intentional or not. For example, when they're giving out instructions, us cats prefer to take them more as suggestions. Things like, 'Stay off the sofa,' or 'Get down from there.'

Craig and Amy's place seemed comfortable enough. They called it a flat, rather than a house. There were no stairs inside and only one bedroom, and they didn't shut the doors, even at night time. Apart from a living room and bathroom, they had a kitchen, and another room with a desk and chair in it. The space was very different from Doug's, but it would do. There was still plenty to explore.

Following a thorough inspection of the flat, I found lots of places to hide. Many feeders lack a basic understanding of feline requirements, often unaware that we must have sufficient personal space. We're not dogs, we don't rely on a constant supply of attention like it's oxygen. Equally, though, we retain the right to demand contact when we need it. There's a fine whisker's breadth between the devoted feeder worship we desire and a downright invasion of our privacy.

Of course, all cats are different. I'm partial to the odd belly-rub when I'm in the right mood, but for the majority of felines, tickling one's undercarriage is a sign of disrespect. We show our bellies to our feeders as a sign of our trust; literally rolling over and displaying our most vulnerable side. For a feeder to take advantage of that and attack us in our weakest spot, abusing our hard-earned trust, is just plain rude. A defensive, claws-out attack is often the only sensible response.

When I needed some napping time alone with no disruptions, I had to find quiet spots the feeders didn't know about. They're cleverer than they look though, some of them. Amy and Craig usually managed to track me down, but there were some useful tight spaces where they couldn't reach me. Even if they could see me, their big feeder arms were too chunky to squeeze in far enough to touch me. So they had to give up and leave me be after a while.

Once, I caught Amy searching for me in completely the wrong place. Sauntering into the kitchen for a drink, I found her lying on the floor, eagerly calling out my name. As if I would want to get covered in the dust and detritus under there! As amused as I was, I heard a spider tremble in her web under a cabinet - an arachnid I happened to know also went by the name of Molly. The poor thing was petrified on hearing a feeder persistently addressing her. So I diverted Amy's attention by making my presence known in the doorway. Amazed I hadn't been under the kitchen cupboards, she looked at me as if I'd just performed some kind of miraculous magic trick. What an idiot.

Sometimes, I liked to hide in the same room as my feeders. That way, I had both the security of knowing they were close by if I needed anything, and the comfort of napping alone. Cardboard boxes that deliveries arrived in always made for great snoozing spots. Not only were they warm in the colder weather and cool in the heat, but the rigid sides protected me from any unwanted intruders disturbing my sleep. One of the many behaviour traits us cats get from our ancestors is the requirement to nap somewhere that provides that kind of protection. As Mummacat used to say, 'You can't be taken by surprise when you're sheltered in a box.'

Occasionally, a delivery arrived with something in it for me. A cosy bed, for example, or a cat blanket. Feeders think us cats' affections can be bought rather than worked for. We won't fall for that trick though, so we tend to shun the gift in favour of the protective packaging it arrived in.

Both the new feeders talked to me a lot, and although Craig sounded similar to Doug, Amy's voice bore no resemblance to Jeanette's. Her accent was more akin to ones that came from the picture box sometimes, on the BBC news and in documentaries. It was strange to hear a real-life feeder pronouncing things in such peculiar ways. Amy's words stretched out as if she was moving her mouth too much as she spoke, and there was a different tune to her sentences; less melodic than Craig's and Jeanette's. I found it confusing to start with. By that time, I'd grown used to the voices from the picture box, and often tuned them out when they weren't discussing a subject of interest. But hearing Amy right there in the room, saying my name rather than reporting on death and disaster, or some game called football, was most peculiar. Craig loved football, but I couldn't understand the fuss. Cats had been kicking balls around for entertainment since time began, but they didn't talk about that in the news. Over time, Amy's voice became normal to me. Not that it really mattered. As I mentioned before, what feeders said was generally neither here nor there.

It turned out Amy and Craig were very compliant and easily trained. I got attention whenever I wanted it, they played with me when I required exercise, and they never pushed me off the sofa. Plus, they went out every day to give me alone time, although not for as long as Doug used to. Each morning and evening, my meals arrived in a timely fashion. The catering was more than adequate, and they shared their own spoils too, when they had something on their plates that was up to my standard.

Since the feeders left the bedroom door open, giving me free access at all hours, I came up with a game to play, to test out their compliance. My aim was to see how early I could get them up in the mornings to feed me. Most nights, I entertained myself in the living room once they'd gone to sleep. What I got up to is my business alone, but needless to say, it left me hungry. The lazy feeders slept for such a long time, I decided they ought to wake up and provide me with breakfast before sunrise. Initially, I chose a time soon before they would normally wake, and when the moment arrived, I set my plan into motion. The best method I found to rouse them to consciousness involved walking over them and sniffing their faces. Amy was easier to disturb than Craig, so she became my prime target. I'd carefully pad up her legs and torso, then brush my whiskers against her face. If she still wasn't responsive, I resorted to shouting. 'Hey! Breakfast time! You're so lazy!' She didn't understand meowlings, so I could pretty much say what I wanted. Within minutes, my perseverance paid off. She'd grumble for a while, but then give in, get up and serve me food.

Each day, I woke Amy a bit earlier, just to see what I could get away with. After a week, the feeders started giving me snacks late at night too, before they turned in for bed. They wanted to keep my belly full for longer, but I wasn't stupid. However, it became harder to wake Amy in the mornings as she became wise to my plotting. Instead of getting up and feeding me in the dark hours, she objected and pushed me away. Eventually, she grew really stubborn, so I had to declare my experiment over and focus my energy elsewhere.

The only access to the outside was via the door that Amy and Craig disappeared through every day. It was the same door I'd been carried through when I first arrived. Back then, I was scared I wouldn't be able to walk on grass again, or smell the outdoors, like that tortoiseshell in the tower. I figured my visit would be over soon though, and besides, I'd got used to being indoors. I had all the attention I needed, plus enough me-time, and there was plenty of fresh air breezing in through the windows.

Sometimes, when Craig disappeared for a full day, he would present me with a gift on his return, to make up for his absence. Usually a feather from a large, exotic bird that smelled of crisp air and wild, distant territories. I wouldn't normally accept an offering so readily, but the scent was so alluring, I found it hard to resist. With Craig's assistance, I used the feathers to practise my hunting, so that one day, on encountering the whole bird in flight, I would be able to take it down with a slash of a claw and a swift, sharp bite.

Most days, I found some prey in the flat. A chunk of meat, for example, that I discovered through my exploring skills, or vermin I had killed on an earlier hunt that had completely eluded my memory. I'd tell Amy and Craig all about it, so they could be assured that the house was free of pests. They congratulated me and said I deserved the treat, and once satisfied by their admirations, I hunkered down to consume the well-earned morsel. Occasionally, the strangest phenomenon occurred, and the prey vanished just as I stooped down to eat it. I could only imagine that it had sprung back to life and run away at the crucial moment before its final expiration. A tasty treat disappearing from right under my nose was horribly infuriating. However, I would find it some time later, having succumbed to its wounds from my dagger-like claws.

As days passed in the flat, I expected to be returned to Doug and Jeanette's once they got back from their caravan holiday. But Amy said something about me staying with them forever. I was so comfy on the sofa, I didn't mind.

7. SANDBANK CRESCENT

'When hunting doesn't come naturally, find your greatest strength. In your case, your ability to look cute.' - Mummacat

Since I was going to be staying in the flat, I decided to show the feeders a little more affection. Mummacat taught me that offering a whisker of trust would pay back, as far as receiving treats and favours were concerned. My previous experiences made me cautious, but the older I'd got, the wiser I'd become, and the more Mumma's lessons made sense. I was still honing my skills, and Amy and Craig were perfect case studies.

As a first case in point, I wanted to find out what lay beyond the front door. I just needed to work out how to manipulate the feeders into giving me a guided tour. It turned out to be an easier challenge than I'd anticipated. The trick was in the timing. When one of them was about to pass by, I sat at the end of the hallway and stared longingly at the door, until they got the message. Sure enough, Amy opened it so I could wander out and look around. The outside world had the same blurry edges as the indoors, so I had to rely on my whiskers and smell sensors (I like to call them scentsors) to investigate. The fuzziness didn't bother me. I was born blind, as all kittens are, so my other senses were well equipped to explore without the use of my eyes.

Still settling into the indoors at the flat, I was in no great rush to expand my territory, but since Craig and Amy went out there every day, curiosity got the better of me. The inside provided a perfectly comfortable living space, so I was keen to find out what was so appealing beyond the door. As it turned out, the outside was just as underwhelming as I'd expected. The carpet and walls reeked of other feeders and cleaning products, so not particularly alluring. On the other hand, I found no evidence of other animals around, which had been my main concern. I remained the rightful reigning Princess of the building.

Every day, one of the feeders opened the front door so I could explore a little further. Amy was at home more than Craig, so she usually escorted me on my walks. They both went out to Work, like Doug had, although goodness knows what they all did when they were there. Amy didn't go there as much as Craig, and she spent half her time at home in the room with the desk, staring at a screen that looked like a picture box. It wasn't nearly as entertaining, though, with no tiny feeders or voices blaring out. Lines, words and numbers filled the screen, which Amy manipulated with something she called a mouse, although I checked it thoroughly and it was definitely not from the rodent gene pool. Anyway, in the absence of any actual fun, I installed myself as entertainer-in-chief, sitting on the desk and demanding fur rubs.

Where Craig took off to every day - the allusive Work place - was a mystery, but I'd watch him from the window, leaving the building, getting into his car and disappearing away down the road. Rather him than me. I hated being in those metal boxes. Always stuck in the back, in my carrier, being thrown around and knocked off my paws every few seconds. However, once I started exploring the outdoors, I discovered cars were useful when they arrived into the crescent. Their underbellies stayed warm for ages and provided a decent shelter from the wind and cold weather. I enjoyed whiling my time away, making the most of a freshly driven engine; hidden away from the world and yet able to breathe the outdoors air and feel the tarmac beneath my pads. No predators or enemies could creep up on me while I was tucked behind a wheel.

The firm ground made a change from plush carpets and furnishings, which, although pleasant, after a while felt a little too comfortable. Still an outdoor creature in part, I didn't want my pads to get too soft. I needed to stay prepared for adventures and hunting, as a cat never knows what's around the next corner. Although I loved living with Amy and Craig, I didn't dare to assume it would always be so good. As I knew from experience, circumstances could change like the wind. It only takes a mini-feeder to come along and disrupt everything. Every day, I used my scratching post to keep my claws and senses sharp, and I applied the same logic for keeping my paws tough by sitting outdoors.

Amy didn't like me resting under cars. I'm not sure why. If we weren't walking, she preferred to be indoors, staring at her silent picture box, or making fancy meals with her hunted spoils in the kitchen. As long as we kept moving, she'd be happy, but she quickly got bored when I indulged in my car time. What was it with feeders and needing to keep busy, instead of stopping to appreciate what's around them?

Anyway, just to appease her, I'd move away from the radiating engine and continue to explore the crescent. I felt safe knowing she was close by and we could return indoors whenever we wanted. Every week, the world became blurrier, and I grew increasingly worried about getting lost. Back when I'd been homeless and wandering the streets, I hadn't been scared at all. However, since settling into the flat, and enjoying the comfort and security of my new home, the prospect of losing it was too great a risk for me to take.

Aside from the fear of becoming estranged from Amy, I had only one other concern when out on my walks. My dislike of other cats remained, but dogs terrified me, so I wanted to avoid them at all costs. That's not to say I couldn't hold my own. I could have taken one in a fight. Probably. The only other option was to stay indoors and out of all potential danger, but I didn't see why I should have my freedom restricted. Regular inspections of the wider territory were vital to my sense of security, and given the opportunity to explore, my curiosity always prevailed.

Thankfully, it turned out the crescent was canine-free. The few felines that lived nearby were mostly respectful enough to keep their distance, although, on the odd occasion, I came across an ill-mannered mog who took me by surprise. For example, one sunny spring day, I was busy sniffing the threshold of a neighbouring house, trying to work out who lived there. The scent effusing from the gaps around the door was giving me musky floral perfume and aged skin dust, mixed with wood polish and an interesting choice of plug-in air freshener. Being so deeply engrossed in aroma analysis, my scentsors didn't register a lithe Bengal tomcat creeping up the path. When he got close, his pretentious odour invaded my right nostril, and I almost jumped out of my fur. In fact, if I'd moved any faster, I would have left my entire coat behind. Amy hadn't even been looking. She stood several tails away, facing the other direction, oblivious to the drama unfolding by the door. A fat lot of use, that was! She had one job - as a look-out, to keep me safe - and she'd failed.

As the Bengal made his ill-mannered greeting, I leapt up, screeched in horror and then dashed off, with Amy trailing on after me. I'm sure I heard her apologising to the other cat, who, in turn, sneered at my reaction. The cheek of it! After that episode, Amy behaved a bit more responsibly when other cats were out in the crescent, shooing them off or placing herself between us, allowing me to go about my business undisturbed.

The best outdoor weather was warm and dry. Not too hot, or my dark patches roasted, but blue skies and sunshine with a light breeze was my favourite. In contrast, rain was not my friend. It tapped on my head and back, and played with my whiskers, teasing my sanity. Within minutes, it soaked into my fur and weighed down my coat like a blanket of cold custard. A little fine rain didn't bother me - what Amy called a drizzle - but when big wet drops started falling from the sky, I'd rush back indoors to have a good wash.

The cold was bearable if a car had recently parked in the crescent for me to keep warm under. When I heard one arriving, I'd turn towards the sound, ready to take up position and absorb the engine heat, like a giant overhead feeder lap. But Amy would call me back, or pick me up, saying it wasn't safe and that I'd get run over. I don't know why she was so worried. Did she really think a big metal box could outsmart a cat? There's a silly thought. Anyway, I let her believe she was saving me from some terrible fate, and we'd continue on our walk.

There was only one weather condition I found completely intolerable. Snow. What is that about? Cold and wet at the same time, and solid, so one has to plunge a paw right into it to get anywhere. No, thank you! The first day I experienced it, Amy and I walked down the stairs and along the hallway as usual. As she opened the main door, we discovered the outside world had literally frozen over. The ground was covered in crunchy, biting, damp fluff. Not my bowl of milk. As keen as I was to shelter under a warm engine, I was not prepared to trudge through freezing sludge to do it. Thankfully, the snow only invaded when it was really cold, and I wasn't to see it again for several more years.

An important part of my duties as the feline Princess of the crescent was to know exactly what was what in my territory. So I made a point of visiting every nook, focussing on a different section of the street each day. Each house had a distinct aroma, unique to its occupant. If it had a resident cat, then it stunk to high heaven. It was a strange thing that all other cats reeked and yet I smelled divine.

The outdoor area I liked the most (even more than under cars) was the grass. It was soft and cool and useful to eat. Large banks of green lawn lay behind the buildings on our side, which I spent many sunny days exploring. Sometimes, if I walked further than usual, Amy called out to me to stop. On every trip, I expanded my territory a little more, but she objected if I strayed too far from the houses. She didn't seem to understand that it was my duty as the territorial feline to survey my whole domain.

A road passed along the end of the crescent. I heard cars whizzing past up there, and I wanted to investigate, but Amy wouldn't let me go, even though I would have kept myself out of trouble. Even after several weeks of daily walks, she didn't trust me, which was ironic, given how trustworthy feeders are to cats. She said she wanted me to stay safe, and although I was desperate to explore further, I did rather like her, so I did as I was told, albeit simultaneously making my objections clear. Amy was the one who hunted my food after all, and I guess I knew that, deep down, she had my best interests at heart. Apparently, she saw things I couldn't, and she knew better about the outside world than me. I just wanted to walk close enough to get everything into focus. The world had definitely got fuzzier.

On one beautiful, bright, warm day, a flurry of chattering birds gathered in the air above. Every so often, one dropped to the ground, looking for food. Darting brown blurs bombed down and then swooped straight back up again. Crouching in stalking mode, I prepared my haunches to spring into action when the moment arrived. A tweeter plummeted to the earth, and I pounced; leaping towards it, just as I'd practised in the flat with the feathers that Craig so regularly bounced in front of my face. As my left leg pushed off from the pavement, my hip twinged, limiting my movement, and I missed my target. The bird flew off faster than I expected. It didn't hang around like Craig's feathers did. Another tweeter dived and touched the floor, and I leapt forwards, claws out, jaws ready. But it was gone; missed by a whisker. The next one would be mine. I froze, waiting, in the hope they wouldn't see me if I stayed dead still. Then I felt a flutter above my head, but it didn't land. Instead, the play-things twittered above me before flying away, letting out peals of laughter as they disappeared over the houses. Next time, I'd have them.

I did actually catch a bird once. A big black one. It made the mistake of landing on the ground near me, and it was looking the other way when I took my chance and went in for the kill; slashing feathers and biting flesh until the winged beast surrendered to my superior nature. The battle was a blur, but I was a hero. Once victorious, I resisted feasting on my prey, choosing to save it for later instead. Since my feeders brought my meals, I figured if I caught my own dinner, they might stop hunting for me. So I sat back and admired my handiwork, revelling in the glory. Then Amy came along and said it was time to go. Insisting I moved away, she muttered something about being out for a walk and wasting time under cars. I refused to budge, waiting for her to spot my prey and retract her complaint and instead shower me with praise for my achievement. At last, she saw the expired bird by the far wheel of the car, and she laughed! She didn't believe that I'd killed it! The cheek. Well, she could scoff all she wanted. I knew the truth. My work there was done, so I trotted off after her before she left me behind.

Craig continued to bring me feathers when he came home from his trips away, and I used them to refine my kill techniques for my next twitching opportunity. The feeders brought me other toys too, and I got lots of exercise running around the flat. Hunting mice and chasing fish across the living room were my favourite hobbies. Sometimes I'd be too tired for games, but playing seemed to make the feeders happy, so I'd usually indulge them. The toys disappeared out of my view with surprising speed, so I had to move like lightning to keep up with them. Occasionally I'd run so fast my tracking got thrown out, and I'd bang my head into a piece of furniture. The knock would leave me dizzy for a second, but I'd set myself right and carry on. I'm sure the feeders didn't notice.

After a good playing session, Amy and Craig brought out the special treat bag. When I was a small kitten, Mummacat told me and my kitlings about a type of grass we might be tempted by when we're older. She called it The Nip. She warned us we mustn't sniff it, although she never explained why. At the time, I promised her I wouldn't touch it, but I didn't know how to tell what any treat was without sniffing it first. So, I discovered the illicit Nip grass by accident. As Amy held out the bag of dried leaves, a strange, alluring aroma captured my scentsors. It was like nothing I'd sniffed before, and by the time I realised what it was, its intoxicating scent had lured me in. Mummacat would have told me off if she'd been there, but it smelled so good I was powerless to resist. The temptation was too great.

The feeders dipped their fingers in it and offered them to me, urging me to sniff the forbidden bounty. When it was right there in front of my nose, it seemed rude to refuse it. A big part of me felt terribly guilty, but at the same time, the smell of The Nip made me so relaxed, I didn't really care. Before I had a chance to engage my willpower, I succumbed to the scent, and found I couldn't get enough of the heady fragrance. I wanted to taste it. The feeders let me lick and chew the flavour from their fingers, which infused into my scentsors and up into my brain. I felt so happy and chilled, I forgot all about my headache from running into the table leg, and my worries drifted away. I lay there on the floor for a while, embracing the experience, until I realised I was hungry and went to check my food bowl for crunchies.

Craig, Amy, and I spent our evenings relaxing in the living room. After dinner, they'd watch the picture box while I entertained myself. Sometimes I'd listen in on their programme, if it sounded interesting. Other times, I'd pick a comfy spot and settle in for a much-deserved rest. It's rare to find a snoozing place that's already fit to nap on. Usually, I'd have to make it comfortable first, by adjusting the padding and fluffing it up. For some reason, feeders object to this when the bed in question is their lap. I'd get to work, prepping it to suit my needs, but all too often they shoved me off, or moved my paws. I couldn't understand it. Feeders wore layers of clothes - thick trousers and woolly jumpers - that needed plumping up and squashing down for me to get cosy. Refusing me the right to some basic comfort and vital recharging was, frankly, rude.

The same issue had arisen with Doug, but being new to feline ways, I'd afforded him a little slack. Craig and Amy, on the other hand, I expected better from. They had both talked about being cat allies before. Amy was the least objectionable, so hers was frequently my lap of choice, although she developed a habit of lifting me up and placing a cushion between us. The problem then was the surface would be too soft, and the padding blocked the body heat, which defeated the purpose of napping on a feeder in the first place. If I'd wanted to sleep on any old bed, I could have done that without it being on a pair of restless legs. Feeders plumped their pillows and patted their quilts, so I found the double standard infuriating. Amy gave in though, if I persisted, and let me settle properly, even if she did interfere with my claws in the process.

There was a second reason for padding my paws on Craig and Amy. Scent-marking is a vital process, used to ensure one's feeders are always stamped with a distinct feline ownership. Not that mine needed reminding, thankfully, unlike some other feeders I could mention. I rarely caught any whiffs of betrayal from Amy or Craig. When they visited his parents' house, they came home smelling of other felines, but they never brought them into the house, which was a firm deal-breaker for me. Even when Craig's family came visiting, they were sensible enough to leave their cat allies behind.

Occasionally, Craig and Amy raised their voices to each other. The air would turn hot and then cold, leaving my fur prickling in an atmosphere one could slice with a claw. As usual, it came down to me to step in and diffuse the situation and make them all gooey again. I'd stand in between them and cry, or get Amy to sit by climbing up her leg. When she picked me up, her voice softened as my natural calming powers kicked in. Then the pair of them resolved their differences, or took a break from squabbling, allowing the atmosphere to settled again.

Craig and Amy didn't argue often. Usually, the house was calm and quiet, and I spent my days sleeping, play-hunting and adventuring outdoors. When the feeders were out, though, that was my time. There wasn't much to rebel against in the flat, not like at Doug and Jeanette's place, where I'd sneak into bedrooms or sleep on the furniture in their absence. The new feeders let me nap wherever I wanted, and they even encouraged me to settle on the sofa or the comfy round chair. However, they kept the front door shut, so I couldn't wander outside on my own.

On one particularly hot summer's day, when the air was stiflingly close, my nose caught the breeze, and I realised a window had been left open. The gap was right at the top, but I jumped up and out, landing on the ledge on the other side. The fresh air cutting through the stagnant heat felt glorious. I sat there for a while, contemplating life and the universe, and planning my next adventure. Then I became aware of a commotion behind me in the living room. Craig's arm was waving around, fishing out of the window, trying to reach me as if I needed rescuing! His face pressed up against the glass, a ridiculous panicked expression frozen onto it, his skin squished like roadkill. The only way to calm him down was to go back indoors, so reluctantly, I stretched up, allowing him to reach me and lift me back in. Craig and Amy kept the windows on their latches after that, the spaces left open too tight for me to fit through.

8. MEWVING

'All other species should be treated with caution until they can prove their alliance.' - Mummacat

After a couple of years of normality in the flat, the feeders' arguments became more frequent, and the atmosphere turned ever more frosty as Craig and Amy grew apart. I tried being extra playful and friendly, but it didn't make much of a difference. Eventually, Craig moved out. He was very sad, and I was too. In the months afterwards, I missed the games he played with me. And I missed the fresh feathers from faraway places that smelled of mountains and lakes, like the blurry pictures I'd seen on the walls.

A girl called Cat moved in with us, which I found very confusing. Goodness knows why a feeder would give themselves the label of a whole other species. Every time Amy called out to her, I jumped with fright, thinking she was announcing the presence of another actual cat in the flat.

Amy moved her desk into the living room and Cat-the-feeder put a bed in its place. Despite her name, she had a much more sensible accent than Amy. It was a bit like Jeanette's, but posher. Apparently, she came from Edinburgh. She was friendly and attentive, but she came with her own pet: a small, fuzzy creature with rough hair that reeked of dead grass and cabbage. She called it Toast The Crazy Guinea Pig, although I saw no resemblance to actual toast, and crazy wasn't the word I would have chosen to describe it. The tiny hairy pig didn't interest me, it had no independence. It lived in a cage and snuffled around the floor when Cat-the-feeder let it out. Apparently, its only pastime was chewing up everything within its reach. Many a comfy box ended up with a breeze hole nibbled through from the outside. The silly critter wasn't even toilet trained.

Speaking of toilets, I had a high standard for mine and I insisted my feeders kept it fresh and tidy. To make sure they did this, I gave them good reason to clean it. They thought I was stupid, missing the tray by pooping over the edge, but the act was entirely deliberate. My way of keeping them in check, shall we say? Once again, the feeders lived under the delusion that they were in charge, but I knew better. Amy also thought she had authority over my walks. In reality, I went where I wanted to go, only taking advantage of her company to minimise any potential danger.

The following few months passed pleasantly enough, getting used to Cat-the-feeder being there instead of Craig. There was more room on the bed and the sofa, although feather hunting wasn't the same anymore. I just carried on as normal; eating, washing, napping, and getting Amy to open the door for my walks. The crescent became fuzzier as the seasons changed, but my acute hearing kept me safe. The sound of Amy's footsteps behind me, and her occasional vocal signals, ensured I didn't lose her as I carried out my daily territorial inspections.

Then, one day, Amy announced she was going away and wouldn't be home for a few weeks. She'd gone away before, but that was when Craig lived with us, so I didn't mind too much. Since Cat-the-feeder was new (and therefore untrustworthy until proven otherwise), I thought it very unfair of Amy to abandon me with her like that. She said she had to go for Work, but all the other feeders went to Work too and they came back every day. I couldn't understand why she had to be there for so long, or how Work could possibly be more important than being in the flat with me. Throughout my experience of living with feeders, they'd gone to Work for a few hours each day. Never for multiple days, or entire weeks.

The time Amy disappeared while Craig was still there, I thought she'd left us for good. When she came back, she expected me to be happy to see her. How was I meant to be happy after she'd abandoned us? I was furious. I'd expected Craig to be upset too, but he wasn't, which made no sense at all. For several days, I ignored Amy and stayed out of her way. To her credit, she persisted in her efforts to get me to forgive her, and I had to admit that I'd missed her warm lap and gentle fur rubs. So, after plenty of extra attention and treats, I forgave her and all was well again.

When Amy told me she was abandoning me for a second time, it came as quite a shock. She said she was sorry and that she'd miss me, but why would she go away at all in that case? I had no idea if she really intended to come back, even though she promised me she would. Every part of me, from my nose to my tail, wanted to trust her, but I didn't know what to believe. Feeders had let me down before, and I knew all too well it could happen again.

The flat felt empty without my trusted ally. I wiled away the days in my usual manner, hanging out with Cat-the-feeder and making fun of Toast The Crazy Guinea Pig. Not that Cat or Toast knew about my silent jeering, as I kept a healthy distance from the fuzzy creature, so they'd think I hadn't seen it. But I could smell it. Yuk.

Cat-the-feeder took me out for my walks, as I'd heard Amy ask her to before she left. We were never out for long though, and didn't go far. Cat's trust levels sunk even lower than Amy's.

Amy did come back, of course. Whenever she left, she kept her word and returned eventually. Despite my resentment, I was secretly glad to have her home, and I'd forgive her slightly faster each time. Us felines don't hold grudges, life is far too short for that. Of course, I'd milk it, though, because Amy would always hunt a tasty meal on her return, and indulge me with plenty of guilt-ridden treats and fuss.

One spring morning, Amy's dad came to visit and something really strange happened. Amy, her dad, and Cat-the-feeder started putting things into boxes and taking them out of the flat. At first I thought they were tidying up, or moving things around to clean. But then they took the furniture out too, and before long the whole place was empty. Amid the chaos, Amy put me in my carrier, because she said I was getting in the way, although I'd been merely enquiring about what was going on. As I watched, every one of her belongings was carried away, and my curiosity twisted into anxiety. What were they doing with it all? Was Amy leaving for good? Was she about to leave me behind in an empty house, alone and trapped in my horrid plastic box? No, she wouldn't do that. Would she? I flipped between feeling terrified and reassuring myself that Amy was trustworthy, and settling down again. Then silence overwhelmed me and palpitations came, as I panicked at the thought of being abandoned and forgotten. I called out, but got no reply. Just the hollow echo of a lonely meow in a large, deserted flat.

As the wind changed direction and a breeze blew through an open window, I heard voices and movements outside. Amy and her dad. Car doors opened and closed and, terrified they were leaving me forever, I cried and cried. I tried to escape from the carrier, but in my panic, my claw kept missing the latch. Exhausted, I lay defeated in the crate, contemplating this cruel turn of events. Then Amy's feet appeared before me. I crouched as still as a mouse caught out in the open, awaiting her next move and, with it, my fate. She said something to me, but I was too stressed to take it in, or decipher the meaning. My ears were blocking everything out, as if protecting me from hearing some awful news. Then Amy lifted the carrier and took me out of the flat, just as she had done with everything else.

As we walked out of the building, into the open air, I saw no sign of her belongings. All I could make out through the grill door of the box was a big white car they called a van. Amy opened a door at the front and placed my carrier on the seat. It smelled horrid. A sickly air freshener was failing to cover all manner of stenches. Amy put my crate on her lap so I could see her, but there was nothing else appealing about being in that acrid metal box.

The journey didn't feel like a visit to the V, but I had no idea where we were going, or why. I demanded to be let out of the carrier. Amy knew I hated travelling. I wondered if she was taking me to Work with her, so I wouldn't be angry about her abandoning me. Although she'd never taken the whole contents of the flat to Work before.

For the first part of the journey, the van kept stopping and starting, but after a while, it moved faster and faster. Amy talked to me in a kind, patronising tone, which meant something bad was happening. Her dad chatted too. He had the same sort of accent as Amy did - unlike Craig's or Doug's, although it was soft and strangely reassuring. I didn't want to be taken away, though. I didn't want to be in the van and I didn't want to go anywhere new. All I wanted was to be back in the flat, with Amy and all of the things. No amount of complaining seemed to get through to either of them, they just kept telling me to shush, and saying everything was going to be okay. My trust levels disappeared faster than a shrew in a shrub.

Not knowing how long I'd be trapped in the horrid metal box played havoc with my stress levels. Ever since I was a tiny kitten, I had only been put in cars to transport me short distances: to and from the V, or from one residence to another. The journey in the van felt entirely different. If Amy was taking me to live with a new family, why had she packed up all the furniture? I was sure I heard her say we'd be travelling for a few hours, but it seemed like longer than that already. The smell of the van was making me itchy, but I needed to see just how grotty it was. And what with the world being fuzzy to look at, I needed to get up close and sniff around to gain my bearings. In my view, the least Amy could do was let me explore and find out if the van had any redeeming features.

My persistent objections to being locked up finally worked, as she realised I wasn't going to give in, and did as I commanded, releasing the door of my carrier. Initially, she tried to keep me on her lap, but there was no way I'd be content with just sitting there. The van shuddered and juddered, making me feel ill, even with Amy holding onto me so I didn't go flying. By my logic, the closer I was to the ground, the less I'd get thrown about. So I insisted on getting down and starting my search at her feet.

The van was a peculiar place. Compact. Just seats and floor and nothing else, apart from some old metal plates that Amy's dad stepped on and pushed like a strange feeder foot toy. I didn't understand the game, so stuck to investigating rather than joining in. The curious steel lumps reeked of all sorts of things. Dirt mostly, but also food and chewing gum and dog poop, not to mention the whiff of Amy's dad's sandal-clad toes. That space turned out to be the least alluring part of the van. Not that there were many parts to choose from. Amy objected to my exploring by her dad's feet, but I needed to do my job and check it over for pests and dangers. I reported back that the space was clear, but not somewhere I'd recommend visiting. The area by her feet was marginally less offensive, since it lacked the metal toy plates, but also not worth writing home about. Not that I knew where home was anymore.

An enormous window filled the front wall, and smaller ones lined the sides. Things were whooshing past us at great speed and it made me very uneasy. Cats aren't designed to travel that fast. Not unless we're running or jumping with our own limbs. And by that stage, my days of indulging in such activities were far behind me.

Once satisfied I'd gained a feel for the van, I surrendered to Amy's lap again. I declared it the least uncomfortable place to be, and also the safest, despite the nausea-inducing movement. Plus, it was the most acceptable spot for my scentsors. I still wasn't happy though, and not knowing what was going on was bad for my constitution. The only way to keep myself from hyperventilating was to descend into a trance-like state, and pant to keep my blood flowing. That way, I was able to block out my immediate fears and focus purely on staying alive.

Having lost all track of time, suffering in the ghastly metal box, we eventually slowed down and then ground to a halt. Then Amy and her dad got out and walked away, leaving me behind. Before they went, Amy forced me back into my carrier while giving her patronising chat again. She seemed to think I'd be happier, or safer somehow, in the crate rather than out in the van on my own. 'Give me some credit!' I cried, but she didn't take any notice. I waited until they'd gone and then let myself out. They must have thought I was stupid. Why would I choose to stay locked up in a small box, when I could be slightly more relaxed on the padded seat of the bigger one? Especially since it had stopped moving, allowing me to explore it thoroughly without the worry of getting knocked over. I'm well aware of when I'm safe and when I'm not. I know that if we're going to the V and I'm in the back of a moving car, it's safer to be in the carrier than out of it. If I'm in a blind panic, as I was in the empty flat, then it's probably better for me to be contained, so I can't hurt myself. But right then, with the van at a standstill, I was more calm outside the carrier than in it. So I exercised my right to a little freedom.

Amy and her dad came back a while later and, much to my amusement, were baffled that I'd managed to get out of the crate. Honestly, sometimes feeders don't live up to their brain size. They lifted me out and put me down in a patch of dried-out grass. It wasn't the lush lawn near the flat, though, it smelled nothing like it. Surrounded by exhaust fumes in a mystery location, goodness knows how far from home, my stress levels sky-rocketed.

Once back in the van, I conceded that being on Amy's lap while we whizzed along was the best option I had. At least she was there for me to sit on. When they'd left, I'd wondered if they were ever going to return, or if they were leaving me there forever, stuck in that horrid, grotty, tiny room. Various scenarios flickered through my mind. I might have been rescued by a passing stranger and abandoned in a cat prison again, or I could have ended up with a family with dozens of screaming children. Amy and her dad did come back, of course, so I spent the rest of the journey in a silent protest, while attempting to be grateful for what I had. Only a little of my anxiety was relieved by Amy's lap, though. It was impossible to recharge in such a stressful environment, and I hated every minute of being trapped in that unpleasant moving metal prison.

When the van stopped for the final time and Amy announced we'd arrived, she once again put me back in the carrier. I didn't mind so much that time, because I knew it meant the horrendous travelling ordeal was over and we'd be getting out. I just wanted to return to a semblance of normality. Little did I know that life would never be normal again.

I was hoping we'd gone out for the day with Amy's things, just for fun, and when we left the van we'd be back in Sandbank Crescent, at the flat. Amy and her dad would put everything back where it was meant to be, and all would be well again. Instead, Amy carried me into an entirely different house that smelled like nowhere I'd been before. And the first thing that piqued my scentsors was the stench of other cats. I, of course, smelt normal, but all other animals reeked. Not that feeders notice much of the aroma - their noses only catch the mid-notes of the full range of inhalations. They don't even have scent glands in their mouths like we do. I really don't know how they see themselves as the superior species. Anyway, living with other felines was a hard boundary, and I thought I'd made that clear to Amy right from the beginning. She'd witnessed my reaction to other species when we'd been out walking, and I was under the impression she'd understood my dislike of any other four-legged creatures. I had made an exception for Toast the guinea pig, as it didn't have enough brain cells to pose any kind of territorial threat.

As it happened, Amy took me up a flight of stairs to a flat on the upper level of the house. At least she acknowledged the proper hierarchy by literally placing me at the top. That part didn't reek of the other cats, so I was able to make it my own. I've never felt the need to mark my territory. That's a very uncouth habit, only indulged in by those lacking the ability to pull rank without debasing themselves. Instead, I rubbed my scent on everything I could reach with my face, and relied on the odour of my toilet tray to do the rest.

9. HELLCATS

'Cats are peaceful creatures, but anyone who crosses us will regret it.' - Mummacat

The new flat belonged to Amy's dad, in a place called Malvern. Once my nerves had calmed enough for my scentsors to stabilise, I noticed some distinct differences from Glasgow. The air had a slightly crisper quality for a start, and the water tasted cleaner somehow.

The living space was similar in size to the flat in Sandbank Crescent, but it seemed more compact. I had to pick my way through tight spaces to find suitable snoozing spots, and manoeuvre around obstacles to access each room. Amy's dad was a kind man, but disorganised, and filled his flat with all kinds of objects. Apparently, he was a collector of things. There appeared to be no particular theme, but I learned it was polite to refer to old bric-à-brac as 'vintage collectibles'. Each room was infused with the aromas of ancient books, incense, and vintage dust. They weren't my favourite smells, but were at least overpowering enough to block out the stink of the hellcats that wafted up the stairs.

Amy slept in the back bedroom and her dad's bed was in another, near the front. A small bathroom accommodated my toilet tray, and a lounge had windows over-looking a busy road. By sitting on a pile of books and papers that adorned a desk, I had a good vantage point to gaze out over the street below. The details were a blur, but I caught the movement of the cars and heard them as they whizzed past. A peculiar beeping noise also filtered in from the outdoors. It sounded at regular intervals, and at the same time, the cars went quiet. Then, once the beeping stopped, the engines revved and continued on their way. The strange ritual was a mystery to me.

Before long, Amy disappeared again, and didn't return for some time. It turns out Work can be in different places, it's not just one big feeder hunting ground. They go off to do things called Jobs. It still didn't make any logical sense to me.

Amy's dad and I rubbed along as well as could be expected, but things weren't ideal. Due to the aforementioned hellcats residing on the ground floor, I had no access to the outdoors. There was no option of a route out of a window, and I certainly had no intention of climbing down the stairs, despite Amy's dad's attempts to lure me there. Terrifying scenes from the mini-feeders' favourite Indiana Jones films came to mind, as I imagined myself trapped above a pool of boiling lava, or a sea of flesh-eating bugs. No matter how carefully I trod, venturing to the lower level would have meant entering dangerous established territory, and I'd have to have been dog-stupid to put myself at that kind of risk.

Everything in Amy's dad's house looked just as blurry as Sandbank Crescent had, if not a little more. As a result, I was extra wary of wandering into perilous situations, especially as I didn't have Amy there to protect me. The hellcats' odour gave off a dark, ominous vibe. I sensed there were two of them, and they probably had all sorts of traps at their borderline, set to declare my presence. I'd never lived so close to another feline's territory before. If I stepped a paw out of line, all nine of my theoretical lives would have been doomed.

Amy, in her feeder naivety, had told me the downstairs cats were nice, and even suggested I make friends with them! Fat chance of that. Didn't she know cats at all? Other felines aren't to be trusted, especially in family clans. The pair on the ground floor were related. I could smell it. I'd been separated from my mummacat for a reason. Kitlings aren't meant to live together, and during my years of independence, I'd figured out why. Felines are powerful, superior beings. That's a well-known fact. On our own, we dominate our feeders and they submit to our will. So it stands to reason that, in family packs, the power must be so strong it would present a danger to the feeder race and, therefore, society in general. Just imagine what would happen if a large clowder of cats used their powers all at once. The consequence doesn't bear thinking about. We need feeders to do our hunting so we don't have to. That's fundamental. If us felines group together, we could destroy our own slaves, and with them, the entire social order. I'm quite happy having my food bowl filled and my fur rubbed and living an easy life, even if Amy did keep disappearing for weeks on end. Her dad had a good, solid lap, and he mostly let me recharge on it when I wanted. Having made a comfortable bed in a quiet corner, I spent much of my time there, napping and waiting for Amy to return. Or for dinner.

On one side of the lounge, a huge picture box absorbed Amy's dad's attention through the afternoons and evenings. His choice of programme fell into one of three categories: Sport - usually a game called cricket, which I found to be an auditory sedative; quiz shows that were useful for honing my language skills; or silly situational comedies that made him laugh. Once though, he watched a programme about a V practice, where they were treating animals and making them feel better. A dog named Skip had shattered his pelvis by getting himself run over. Everyone knows dogs are stupid, so I had little sympathy, but Skip was so badly hurt, even I wiped away a little sleep dust when he'd fully recovered at the end. Then there was Missy, the cat, who had something called cancer. It sounded horrible, although Missy looked well enough, and was claiming she felt fine. But the V told her feeders there was nothing he could do and they would have to put her down. I didn't understand what he meant at first. I thought they were going to put Missy down on the floor and let her leave with her family. Instead, they gave her an injection, and she fell asleep. All the feeders cried, which was very confusing, because Amy doesn't cry when I have a nap. It turned out Missy wouldn't wake up again. The V said they had put her out of her misery. Missy hadn't seemed miserable to me. In fact, she'd looked perfectly well. When I realised the V had killed her, I was horrified. I sloped off to my bed and stayed there until suppertime.

....

A very, very old lady lived on the ground floor with the hellcats. Occasionally, she climbed up, one slow step at a time, carefully balancing on her ancient wobbly legs, while calling out in a crackling, shrill voice. Somehow she knew my name, and she screeched it out as she gradually made her way, clinging to the bannister and waving her other hand around. I wasn't sure of her intentions, but it crossed my mind that she might have been bringing me treats. After all, she was a feline-trained feeder - albeit befriended by the spawn of the cat-devil. Cautiously approaching her on the landing, I sniffed for any sign of gifts, but all my scentsors caught on the air between us was vintage skin-dust, talcum powder and the stink of the evil hellcats. Their stench clung to her, their hairs and scent-markings shedding from her clothes like acid rain. Realising she must have had duplicitous designs, I hissed at her until she hobbled away again.

Treat offerings from Amy's dad were sparse. Occasionally he'd bring some chicken or ham from somewhere called Co-Op, but he was something called vegetablearian, which apparently meant he didn't eat meat! Just as I thought I'd got feeders sussed, they'd go and do something completely nonsensical. Amy had left him in charge of hunting for me. Did she expect me to live off carrots? He still served my regular meals that came out of packets, so that was a saving grace. When my nominated feeder was out of sight, I'd be alerted by the crinkle and zip of a food pouch opening. It was a sound I'd stored in my brain that I could sense from three rooms away. Like the noise of a traditional can cracking open. All my food used to arrive in cans, so every time I heard the metallic crank of an opener, or the rip of a tin lid coming off, I'd be there, quick as a roach. Increasingly, the contents wasn't offered to me, but I'd perform the ankle dance just in case. Brushing up against legs and winding around ankles usually elicited a tasty treat; tuna being my favourite. And chicken. And beef, or pork, or lamb.

I also brushed up against Amy's dad to scent-mark him for when he went downstairs. He had no choice about entering the hellcats' territory, having to walk through it to go hunting. So I passed the message on for the evil felines to stay away from my floor. It worked, they didn't come near.

On two separate occasions, Amy's dad took me out of the house. This involved going downstairs and passing through the hellcats' flea-pit, for which he coerced me into the dreaded carrier. Although I had no desire to leave the flat without Amy, I was, for a change, grateful for the protection of the plastic box. I crouched at the back of it, hoping the hellcats wouldn't leap up at me. Their stench intensified as we descended the stairs, and I did my best not to allow the acrid stink into my nostrils. At the bottom, we had to pass along the hallway. I squeezed my eyes tightly shut, choosing complete blindness over the shock of a hellcat appearing at the grill door. Thankfully, Amy's dad held me up high off the ground, out of reach of any surprise pounces. He said something to the old lady as we passed by, and then I heard the creak of the front door opening. A few seconds later and cool, fresh air hit my face. We'd made it. The door clicked closed behind us and we were officially out, beyond the threshold of the toxic hellcat territory. Phew! But then panic set in, as I had no idea where I was being taken.

That first time we left the house, we ended up at the V. Since my arrival at Amy's dad's flat, and with very little to do, I discovered a talent I didn't know I had. Somehow, I managed to develop a new appendage on my back. It was a growth of expanding proportion, protruding from my large tabby patch. Firm yet squidgy, it mutated every day, and I was excited to find out what it would become. I could just about reach the lump when washing my hindquarters, and the bigger it grew, the more I was able to tend it. I nurtured it with pride, preening the area carefully and encouraging its development.

When Amy's dad took me to the V, they seemed concerned about it. The man in the white coat prodded and poked at my back, and then produced a needle and stabbed my precious growth, right in the middle! I tried to protest and tell them it was my special lump. But Amy's dad held me down and said things that were meant to soothe and calm me, although unsurprisingly, they didn't work. The V's needle sucked my appendage away, shrinking it down to nothing and leaving me with an empty bag of skin sagging under my fur. Devastated by my loss, I was left deeply upset with Amy's dad for colluding in the plot to destroy what I'd been so tenderly nurturing. Made from my own flesh and blood, and nursed into life by my healing tongue, they had no right to remove my dear lump. They returned me to the carrier while I was still in shock and unable to argue; feeling like I'd literally had the life sucked out of me. Besides, I didn't want to be on that hard white table in that horrid sterile place any longer than I needed to. I resolved to re-grow my lump, bigger and stronger than before.

Amy's dad carried me out of the V and walked back towards the flat. The beeping noise I'd heard so often from behind his window sounded at an alarming pitch, and we crossed the road while the cars had stopped. Next came the piercing metallic squeal of the garden gate that announced the arrival of house visitors. For the second time, then, the visitor was me. As we walked up the pathway, I realised we were about to re-cross the hellcats' stinking territory. My fur stood on end, reflexively puffing up to make me look bigger, as I slipped into defence mode. It was all too much. Having valiantly coped with being taken out of the flat against my will in the first place, I'd bravely survived a traumatic trip to the V. Then, just when I thought the worst was over, I had to deal with passing through the pit of hell once again.

I cowered as far back in my box as I could, closed my eyes, and shut down my scentsors. Amy's dad turned the key in the front door lock and the sound of wood brushing against carpet signalled the darkness before the dawn. My guardian then very loudly announced that we were back. I wanted to yell at him to not draw attention to the fact that I was in the house again, but it was too late. A thud of paws hitting the ground in the room next door set my whiskers on edge. The old lady screeched over the racket from the picture box, 'Is that you, Simon?' It hadn't occurred to me Amy's dad had a name of his own.

'I'll be in in a minute. I'm just taking Molly back upstairs.' Hurry up and get on with it, I thought. I resisted saying it out loud, as I didn't want the hellcats to hear me. Willing him to take me up to the safety of the flat as quickly as possible, I held my breath to keep out the stench. But I could sense a feline nearby, emerging from a door to the right. 'Hello Sparkle,' said Simon.

'Who's in the carrier?' said the hellcat. Amy's dad would have heard it as 'Meouw'.

'You'll get your breakfast in a minute,' he replied. 'I'm taking Molly upstairs first.' He'd stopped moving while he spoke to the hellcat, whose name Sparkle had come as somewhat of a surprise. At a stand in the hallway, we'd paused in the middle of the evil cats' territory.

I silently pleaded for Amy's dad to walk on and take me away up the stairs. Instead, I felt my crate lower towards the floor and slowly turn, so the grill door faced the direction Sparkle had meowed from. Paws padded stealthily towards me. Remaining motionless, I prayed that Sparkle couldn't see me in the shadows of my carrier. I gritted my teeth in anticipation of the solid base making contact with the ground. It didn't, though. The box stopped, mid-air, suspended like a toy dangling from a stick, teasing the keen hunter. A telltale whisp of feline scentsors sniffing the air echoed around my plastic walls, as Sparkle's laser eyes burned into my fur. Her feminine energy swirled around my carrier like a storm brewing. I held my eyes tightly shut, reasoning that if I didn't open them, the hellcat couldn't hurt me. I had to resist the impulse to look, or to associate with her in any way. It was my only chance to remain safe.

'Do you want to say hello?' Simon split the tension, but also induced a state of panic, making me feel suddenly nauseous. I wasn't sure who he was aiming his question at, but I responded with a low growl. As I did so, I opened my eyes. Not intentionally, but a part of me needed to see what sort of danger I was in, even though the rest of me didn't want to know. I looked straight ahead. The yellow grill door dominated my vision, blocking out the world beyond. Re-focusing past the metal, I recognised carpet, walls, and a hallway. No cat. Definitely no other animals in my view. Either Sparkle had invisibility powers, or she'd gone; lost interest and skulked away. Then my carrier raised up into the air again and swung around towards the stairs. Amy's dad was taking me up to the flat, at last. He let me out on the floor of the landing and I rushed to my bed in the corner of the back room. I wished and wished for Amy to come home.

10. MEWVING (AGAIN)

'A cat's affections cannot be bought with fancy beds or blankets. Put your feeder in their place by sleeping in the box instead.' - Mummacat

Time passed slowly in Simon's flat. Once in a while, Amy would return, give me cuddles and treats, and then leave again before I'd had the chance to forgive her for her last desertion. If she wasn't happy staying there for more than a few days, I couldn't see why I should be expected to. But she always said she'd come back, and I kept her at her word. She hadn't let me down before.

In the meantime, I slept and ate and chilled out with her dad. Occasionally, he played with me, but mostly I snoozed on his lap. Sometimes he went out, but otherwise he split his time between our flat and the ancient lady in the hell pit downstairs. When he was down there, I would hear them through the floor, shouting at each other. They weren't arguing, but the picture box was always blaring out so loudly they had to raise their voices to make themselves heard. Why they didn't just turn down the volume and speak normally, I don't know.

'Here's your dinner.'

'What is it?'

'Prawn curry.'

'Oh, lovely! I haven't had prawns in years.'

'You had some yesterday.'

'Did I? Can you turn the tv up? I can't hear it.'

'It's really loud already!'

'I can't hear it. And change the channel, would you? I've seen this before. It's a repeat.'

'Mother, it's the news!'

Eventually, Amy returned from several weeks away and announced that we were moving homes again. She promised she wouldn't leave me after that if she could help it. It didn't bother me where we were, as long as I had her there every day. Being a feeder is a full-time responsibility, and she seemed to have lost sight of that. First, though, she took me to the V. With no warning, she ushered me into the carrier, and I assumed we were leaving for the new home. So, as we passed through the hell pit, I didn't flinch. I looked straight ahead through the grill door, holding my head high, ready to hiss at the hellcats and tell them good riddance.

A few minutes later, and much to my surprise, we were at the V! For a moment, I thought I was there to get my growth seen to, although it hadn't been long since the last cruel deflation. Despite my insistence that it wasn't to be removed, he'd petted me tenderly and said some kind words before sucking it away. This time, however, my lump was still in its preparation stage, having not yet re-grown to its former glory. So, instead of stabbing me in the back (physically and metaphorically), the V injected something into my neck. Suddenly I was a kitten again, and in the Vs surgery for the very first time. The man in the white coat, who smelled of latex gloves and breath mints, pinched the skin behind my head, like Mummacat used to when she told me off for straying too far. The grip paralysed me while he jabbed the needle in. I stretched out my paws, trying to bat him away, but it was futile, as he was just out of my reach.

I don't even know why he did it. In the picture box, feeders got injections when they weren't feeling well, but in real life they seemed to do it to cats just to prove they could. Clearly, it's a ritual intended to exert their misguided sense of superiority over us. Hence, starting when we're kittens. It's a threat they ingrain right from our earliest days of existence. No wonder we all dread a trip to the V.

After that particular injection, I had to endure the humiliation of being taken back through the hell pit, having given the hellcats a piece of my mind only twenty minutes earlier. Thankfully, Amy took me straight upstairs with no dawdling. She left me in my carrier in the flat and I came over all relaxed and drowsy. A thought occurred to me that perhaps the V had actually been a warlock, and he had cast a spell over me, or injected me with a magic potion. I didn't want to sleep, I was scared I wouldn't wake up again. But then something really odd happened.

The door of my carrier fell open, and the carpet started to move. At first it gently vibrated, and then undulated, lifting from the floor in waves. I lay there, watching, aghast, at the scene unravelling before me. Strangely, it was all in perfect focus, which made the whole experience even more terrifying. A bulge the size of a hedgehog grew up from under the ground; rising and stretching bigger and bigger like a giant molehill. Then the carpet tore open right down the middle. Out of the rupture burst the hellcats, swiftly followed by an army of rats and mice. They came for me. Hundreds of eyes shining like torches, sharp teeth glinting and claws extended. I pounced out of my box and took them on, fighting them off one by one. First, I advanced on the rats, slashing and biting, while whipping the mice away with my tail. One of the hellcats came at me with a snarl, but I jumped up on a table and knocked off a vase. Flowers filled the air as the pot smashed over his head, leaving him limp on the floor.

The surviving rodents fled as porcelain shards showered over them and rose petals scattered around the hellcat corpse. Sparkle was my last remaining nemesis. Realising she faced the same fate as all the rest, she looked at me with pure terror in her eyes. Fervently searching around the room, she spiked a white hanky with a claw and waved it about in the air. 'I surrender!' she cried and declared the battle lost. Victory was all mine. I finally had the freedom of the hellcats' territory.

Half-waking in a daze as my carrier jolted this way and that, I found myself on Amy's lap, in a car. The scent structure in the air matched her dad and his vintage collectibles. Exhausted from the battle, I dozed as the engine purred away around me, like a Mummacat cocoon. The journey felt never-ending. As I drifted in and out of sleep, I became aware of music playing, chatter about the traffic, and the patter of rain hitting the windows while the sound of wet roads slooshed by outside.

When the car eventually stopped, we had arrived at our next home at the start of a whole new adventure. Amy placed my carrier on a bed while she and her dad slowly surrounded me with our things. I stayed in the box, snoozing, until my energy returned, and then Amy let me out to explore. Familiar belongings covered every inch of the floor, except for a narrow corridor of carpet through the middle. Amy's desk, the big round red chair, various cardboard boxes, her clothes, my bed and toys. I picked my way through, sniffing every item to check it was in order. Then I came to a doorway, which lead out to an entrance hall, followed by an entire house to explore. At the end of the hallway, I found a room with a sofa and table in it, and after that, a kitchen, which I later discovered, led to a garden. There were also stairs and more rooms to investigate at the top. It was altogether more roomy than Amy's dad's flat, and best of all, there were no hellcats keeping me stuck in my quarters.

Two new feeders shared the house with us, which I found out was in a place called Colchester. The live-in landlord wasn't around much, but seemed friendly enough when he was. Then there was a girl whose way of talking sounded even stranger than Amy's. Her voice was clipped and harsh-sounding; not like anything I'd heard from the picture box. She was nice to me, though, and I worked out most of what she said. Although generally happy to rub my fur and chat, she was less pleased when I sat on her lap; grumbling about my hair on her trousers and saying she had to keep them clean for Work. I felt sorry for feeders who had to go to Work and pretend they didn't live with a cat. What was there to be ashamed of? Fur is far prettier than skin, and it keeps you warmer. I thought she might have been pleased I was sharing it with her. Instead, I left her gifts of it at night time, by sleeping on her bed while she was out.

My toilet was located in the hallway, which although

conveniently close to our bedroom, was a little exposed and unhygienic. The feeders had a whole room dedicated to their personal care, so I didn't understand why I wasn't deemed worthy of the same. To her credit, Amy swapped out my toilet tray for a new covered box, which provided me with my own tiny cubicle. It was enough for me, since I had no use for the running water their bathrooms provided. Felines are self-sufficient when it comes to keeping clean. We don't need fancy facilities to keep ourselves smelling fresh and looking our best.

....

When I discovered the exit to the garden, I was thrilled. A cat-sized, permanently open portal to the outdoors had been built into the kitchen door, allowing me to come and go as I pleased. The weather was warm and there was grass to roll about in and regurgitate. Best of all, I didn't need Amy to let me out, and she didn't consider it necessary to follow me around, encouraging me back in before I was ready. Don't get me wrong, I loved having her there to make sure I could always find my way back. She often sat outside while I pottered about, and left me to my exploring. The garden was bordered by hedges and fences, so there was no risk of getting lost. Outside was peaceful and calm, and all my own territory.

The house quickly felt like home, and within a few weeks, I felt settled and content. Every afternoon, I strolled around the garden on my regular security inspection. On one particular day, I made my way to the kitchen as usual, but I arrived at the back door to discover my outdoor portal had vanished! Completely gone. In its place was a hard plastic shell. Apparently, Amy, or one of the new feeders, didn't want me going outside anymore. I saw no reason at all for them to stifle my freedom. Taking away my access to the outdoors was a breech of my feline rights and I was about to start a noisy protest when Amy appeared and tried to calm me down.

'What is this?' I cried. 'What's going on?'

'It's okay Molly, it's a cat flap.'

'A cat flap? What's that? What happened to my gap? My personal portal to the outside? Put it back immediately!' Amy wasn't listening. She talked over me, saying something about pushing it, and still being able to go out. I had no interest in her excuses. All I wanted was to get to the garden, just as I had before. I knew that if I sat there for long enough, waiting and complaining, something would be done about it. Amy fiddled with the plastic 'cat flap' - presumably trying to remove it for me - and occasionally I caught a draught of fresh air. But as soon as I thought she'd taken the offending barrier away, she put it straight back again. It was like she was teasing me with it, showing me it was some kind of door. She knew I didn't operate doors. That's what she was there for. One moment, she opened it to show me the outside was still there, but then she closed it again, so I couldn't go through. Why was she was being so mean? Her behaviour was highly irregular. Whatever her excuses, it felt deeply unreasonable. Eventually, she held the plastic flap open long enough for me to step out, and I made my escape to the garden.

Amy's strange new door behaviour became the norm for a couple of days, teasing me before letting me out. Sometimes she physically picked me up and rudely cat handled me through the flap. After a while, though, I realised I could play her at her own game and move it myself. If she thought she could control my freedom, she had another thing coming. Very quickly, I learnt to make the plastic flap open with my head, regaining full access to the garden. That taught her.

11. DEAN

'Just because feeders can't understand our meowlings, they assume we're not clever enough to understand them. Idiots.' - Mummacat

I enjoyed our time in that house. The atmosphere was calm and quiet, there were several beds to choose from for my naps, and I got plenty of attention. I had the place to myself most daytimes, so I explored, hunted and slept. When she was home, Amy cooked our spoils, relaxed in the garden with me, and socialised with our housemates. We settled into a comfortable routine, and life was easy.

Then Dean came into our lives. He started visiting for dinner and, before long, he was there almost every day. The bottom half of his face was covered in long, coarse fur. I felt sad for him, that his hair wasn't as silky soft as mine, so I did my best to help him keep it in tip-top condition. Grooming was a serious business though, and he wouldn't stay still - jerking his chin away and complaining that it tickled.

I began to feel poorly around that time, with pain and discomfort in my abdomen. Amy thought I was being naughty, peeing outside my toilet box, but she should have known I wouldn't deliberately soil the floor. It was the only way I could communicate my illness and, as far as I was concerned, my very unsubtle signal clearly indicated a problem with my urinary system. She didn't take the hint, but I managed to get the problem under control myself, with sheer willpower and self-discipline.

A few months later, we moved, yet again, to another home. This time Dean came to live with us too, although the other two feeders stayed behind. I didn't understand the compulsion to move around so much, instead of deciding where to be and staying put. Not that it really bothered me, actually, because as long as I had Amy there, I was perfectly happy. I wouldn't have wanted to go back to Doug and Jeanette's house, or the one before that, with all the mini-feeders. Wherever I lived with Amy, I had free rein of the territory, except for the garden sometimes. And this was one of those times.

The new home turned out to be another flat; all on one level and half the size of the house. And, as I mentioned, there was no cat flap to the outdoors. I tried pushing the door in the kitchen when nobody was looking, but it wouldn't budge. Amy and Dean let me into the garden when I asked, but sometimes mini-feeders played out there, so on those occasions I preferred to stay indoors, in peace. One of the little feeders lived in the building next to us, and when they were outside they would leave their kitchen door open. Naturally, I'd go in for a nose around. Their flat smelled funny, like sour milk and baby wipes, although at least it didn't stink of other felines. Instead of being softly carpeted, their floors were hard and slidey, and gave off a strong whiff of disinfectant. Each room was scattered with toys too big for me to play with, like in my first home. All in all, the neighbour's flat held little interest for me, but it was important I had the lay of the land and regularly inspected my wider territory.

In the early days of living there, Dean and Amy were at home for less than half of their waking hours. Either out at Work, or for dinner, or out with friends, they frequently left me alone in the flat. It was fine, because I was great to be around, but I preferred it when they were there, too. As the months passed, Amy stayed at home more than Dean, and I saw less and less of him. He'd get back late from Work, often returning in the middle of the night, when most feeders were sleeping.

Speaking of sleeping, I could never get my head around why feeders snooze for so many hours in one go. Catnaps are definitely the best way to break up the day, so one can be alert when needed. Feeders sleep for an inordinately long time, wasting precious moments in the dark when the night creatures are out playing. And then they get tired and grumpy in the evenings because they've been awake for so long! It makes no sense to me. I tried to help Amy understand this once, waking her up at intervals, to show her what she was missing out on. I thought if she could grasp the concept of 'little and often' when it comes to rest, it would transform her life. But it didn't work. She got very angry with me and refused to listen, eventually sending me flying across the room one night. So I didn't try again. It was her loss.

Dean had some funny, if infuriating, habits. He was nice to me most of the time, but he also liked to play tricks. For example, he'd let me recharge on his lap, but if I attempted to adjust the padding, he'd tense his stomach to make the surface hard, leaving it impossible to plump.

Another habit he found hilarious involved talking to me as if I were a feeder; chatting away like he was interested in my day, and pretending to understand my responses when I knew full-well he didn't. Plus, he always wanted to have the last word in the conversation. So, I'd call him an idiot, and make sure I got the final meow in, every time.

'Alright Molly, how's it going.'

'Not bad thanks, are you serving breakfast soon?'

'Oh really? What are your plans for today?'

'You don't understand what I'm saying, do you?'

'Interesting. Well, I'm off to Work now.'

'Idiot.'

'I'll see you later.'

'Idiot.'

'Bye.'

'Idiot.'

'You can stop replying now.'

'IDIOT!'

Amy and Dean were really happy together for the first few months in the flat, but over time, the atmosphere grew tense. Arguments became more frequent, and although I was always ready to intervene and pick up the pieces, there was only so much I could do when Amy got upset. Stroking me calmed her and lifted her mood, so I'd sit on her lap or climb up her chest, purring loudly and licking her face to stop the tears.

Sometimes I tried helping her with the housework. Every week she'd change the bedsheets, and I'd offer my services. But she seemed to think I got in the way, and she'd move me off the duvet while I was trying to straighten it or hold it in place for her.

Gradually, my urinary problems returned and became too uncomfortable to hide. I tried to inform my feeders the same way I had before, by peeing away from my tray. Eventually Amy understood, and I gritted my teeth through a trip to the V, knowing they were my only chance to get the problem fixed. I turned to Bastet, praying for my safe return, and she came through for me, as the dreaded words 'put her out of her misery' didn't pass the V's lips. Instead, she advised Amy to serve me a different diet, and being so pleased to have avoided being put down, or forced to take medicine, I ate the food with relish. It helped that Amy specially chose the jelly variety, knowing I couldn't stand the gravy option. When faced with the brackish, watery gloop, it reminded me of the awful prison, and made me feel quite nauseous. Even the dry, meaty chunks under the jelly version gave me occasional flashbacks to that traumatic time, so I usually licked off the sweet, tasty coating and left the rest, unless I was starving.

Amy also changed my water bowl to a fancy moving fountain. At last, my feeders had started to understand the feline preference for fresh water, rather than drinking from stagnant troughs. They draw their drink from a tap rather than partake from a glass that's been sitting around for days, so why us cats should be expected to do that mystifies me. At least I knew Amy's personal supply had been refreshed within the previous few hours, so I took any opportunity to drink from that over my own dirty dish.

Amy and I spent our evenings relaxing together while Dean was out at Work, and I'd be her bed companion when he didn't come home. More often than not, when he did, he reeked of alcohol. I know that, as a feline, my tastes are broad compared to a feeder's, but alcohol was a step too far for me, and sweaty beer breath is not an alluring scent.

We lived in the flat for over a year, with ups and downs, and arguments and reconciliations. Eventually, Amy and Dean put their differences aside, and we moved home again. Amy said it would be a fresh start for all of us. She was clearly hoping to improve her relationship with Dean, but I knew it would take more than a change of scenery. The new house wasn't a long drive away, and it smelled familiar; reminiscent of the last one we'd stayed in, with the nice housemates. I could sense we weren't far from there. Not that I had any particular desire to return. It had been a lovely place to live, but there's no point looking backwards in life. The here and now are all that matter.

The new house had much more going for it than the flat. It was large and spacious, with lots of rooms to explore, and a proper garden again. I got to know it mainly through smells and sounds and using my whiskers, since everything past my paw blurred into a mash of colours and vague shapes. I wondered if it was the same for Amy, or if her eyes adapted. The fuzziness was unnerving, but it wouldn't stop me finding my way around.

I got to know the height of furniture through trial and error, and once I knew how high I was from the floor, it was easy enough to get back down again. However, Dean liked to tease me by lifting me up onto a platform. Aware I didn't know how far it was from the ground, he revelled in the fact that I couldn't simply jump back down. Memories of my accident with the wall flashed through my mind, warning me not to take the risk. Usually, I'd find a step below by reaching out a paw, but Dean put me on a surface with no obvious access back to the ground. As I focussed on fishing for a foot-hold, I'd hear him sniggering nearby, but Amy would be there too, and she'd get me down after a while. I could always rely on her to come to my rescue.

12. HOLBY KITTY

'Don't be tempted by The Nip, it has been the downfall of many a respectable cat.'

- Mummacat

The lump I carefully nurtured disappeared every so often. Sometimes Amy would take me to the V and have it deflated with a needle. Other times I'd scratch it accidentally, on a low branch, or when I rolled around in the garden. All my efforts, ruined. I hated going to the V. They didn't understand that I'd grown my lump deliberately; that perhaps one day it would be useful. It could be an extra tail, or maybe develop claws for hunting birds with. When Dean or Amy treated me to a pinch of Nip, I came up with all sorts of ideas for what my appendage might do. Especially when the picture box was showing Frankenstein, or Edward Scissorhands. Anyway, although I despised the V for destroying it, at least their method was relatively painless. The times it burst while I was adventuring, my back ended up feeling sore and it took a lot of washing to fix it. The more my skin got damaged, the harder work it was to repair, and it became increasingly uncomfortable. I started to suspect it may not be possible to grow it into something practical after all. However, I had no intention of giving up. I was a glass half full kind of cat. That is, until I found the glass, and then it would be nearly empty.

One day, Amy took me to the V when my lump was just starting to re-grow. Each time it developed, it grew a little bigger, before, one way or another, it disappeared again. On this particular occasion, while at less than half its potential size, I was still in the process of nursing it into existence. So I couldn't understand why Amy was taking me to the horrid V. As I cowered on the table, conversations floating over me like an ominous fog, I braced myself for the woman in white to produce a needle. She didn't, though. Instead, she ushered me back into my crate. She must have realised there wasn't enough of a lump to drain away. Relieved at the thought of going home to relax for the rest of the day, I settled in for the ride. Then, to my horror, the V - not Amy - picked up my carrier and started moving me out of the room, in the opposite direction to the door we'd arrived through. In stunned silence, I watched my feeder bidding me goodbye - just like the day I was taken away from my beloved Mummacat - and I was whisked off in another direction.

The V swept along a corridor and then came to an abrupt halt, pausing to turn a key in a lock. As she pushed a door wide open and stepped through, the atmosphere shifted, as if we were entering another dimension. The bright, sterile air of the hallway turned dark with the acrid stench of sick and scared animals. Crates and cages lined the walls. I couldn't see the occupants, but I didn't need to, as the clamour of upset and distress overwhelmed my scentsors. The knot in my gut felt horribly familiar. My carrier door opened, and the V grabbed me by my scruff, pulled me out, and lifted me into a cage. A fleeting thought of a cat, or some other obnoxious creature already at home in the pen, filled me with dread. Being forced to share such a confined space would have finished me off. To my relief, the cell was otherwise empty. A blanket I recognised from home was placed next to me, and my scentsors filled with comforting aromas. Beyond that, everything was scarily unfamiliar. Panic rose through me, causing my fur to stand on end and my chest tightened.

The last time I'd been caged up was after my accident, before Doug had taken me in. Although admittedly less traumatic than the cattery, it had been stressful enough, and not an experience I had any desire to repeat. I thought I'd seen the last of places like that. I saw no reason to be back in a cat prison, even if it was in a V's practice. Amy hadn't mentioned the word 'holiday'. Was she giving me away? Was I homeless again, and waiting for another family to adopt me? As far as I was concerned, we had a good relationship, and besides, she'd told me many times that she would always be there for me. I'd told myself not to trust her, and now she was proving me right. All feeders showed their true treacherous colours in the end.

As I was concocting a plan to escape from my new hellhole, a different V opened the cage door and coaxed me out. I didn't want to go, but knew I had no choice. Plus, she smelled of treats. She carried me back out to the sterile corridor and through to a white room. At least it was quieter and cleaner than the prison, although I was terrified of what was about to happen. Where was Amy? Despite discovering her deception, I never really believed she would desert me. The V lady rubbed my fur and talked to me softly and calmly, in a way that only meant bad things were imminent.

My instinct was to run away, but there appeared to be no clear route out of the room. The door on the far side was shut, and I heard the one behind us click closed once we were in. The V's white coat smelled of other cats and dogs. Were they the same ones in the prison, screaming and crying? Or were they different creatures; pets she had 'put down', like in Amy's dad's picture box? The thoughts spinning around in my head overwhelmed me. The V said everything would be okay, which is never what I want to hear. I reminded myself that I'd always survived trips to the V before, even when I didn't have a home. I missed Amy and wanted it to be over, whatever 'it' was going to be.

As it happened, it was over with pretty quickly. The nurse jabbed me with a spike and I came over all sleepy, like I had before the last long car journey. Poor Missy came to mind, and I worried I was being put to sleep permanently. And then I blacked out.

When I woke up, it took me a moment to register that I was back in the cell in the prison room. Dazed, groggy, and dry-mouthed, I sniffed out the direction of my water dish. As I lifted my head, I felt a strange pressure on my neck. I froze in fear, in case the grip tightened. Amy had put a collar on me once, but I objected so ferociously she removed it not long afterwards. This was different, though. It wasn't tight all the way around, just in a few places, and it adjusted position as I moved. But I couldn't stay still forever, and I was gasping for a drink. Slowly and carefully, I stood up. The weird restraint loosened its grip as I raised my head, although it continued to cling on as I nervously lapped at my water. Whichever way I looked, the thing encroached on my peripheral vision; it was a semi-solid, semi-opaque circle of plastic that surrounded my head like a halo, slipped from its usual position above my head.

One of the children in my first home had put clothes and a hat on me once, but this didn't feel like a fancy dress situation. The solid halo was similar to a bonnet, but sturdy, and not in the least bit cute. It framed my hazy vision and made everything sound strange and muffled. Noises bounced off the surface and echoed around my head.

A nurse brought me dinner and encouraged me to eat, but I had no appetite. Trying to recall the last thing that happened, I had flashbacks of being drugged and thinking the V was putting me down. Suddenly, I felt really happy to be alive. Then I remembered where I was, and hopelessness set in again. Why had Amy taken me to get locked up? It made no sense when there was nothing wrong with me. I was reminded of Missy again, and how she thought she was fine, but the feeders decided her health was so bad they had to put her out of her misery. They hadn't put me down, so what had they done? And why did I have that annoying hardhat thing on my head? Once again, a sense of dread flashed through me as I worried about being experimented on. My lump itched, and I wanted to lick it. I'd missed at least one of my regular nurturing sessions, and I couldn't reach my back because of the restraint. I tried and tried, but I ran out of energy, so I gave in and licked some jelly off my food instead.

The other animals in the prison spent all day crying and complaining, and the cacophony gave me a headache as it bounced around the horrid hat. Nobody in the room knew why they were there. A shrill Siamese yowled in a pitch that only a Siamese can, bluntly objecting to being locked up and demanding to be let out. As much as I wanted my freedom too, it was pointless crying about it, and even if I did, I couldn't possibly compete with her for volume. The noise brought with it memories of losing my voice in the cattery and I knew it was better for me to keep quiet this time. Besides which, I lacked the energy to muster a meow.

A gruff male moggy attempted to silence the Siamese, complaining that he was trying to nap, and telling her to stop getting her whiskers in a twist. It didn't help, though. A mewling teencat joined in the chorus, ramping up the caterwaul. Finally, a nurse arrived and settled everyone with treats and fur-rubs and calm words. As she opened the door to leave, I heard a dog barking in another room. The poor thing sounded pained and angry. I hid behind my blanket and hoped Amy would come and rescue me before anything really bad happened.

The nurse went home, replaced by a night-shift feeder, and I surrendered to the realisation I that I wouldn't be leaving any time soon. I slept as much as I could, trying to block out the noise, but it was hard, being naturally active in the dark hours. The night nurse gave me some medicine that numbed my pain and made me even more woozy, allowing me to nap.

When dawn broke, more feeders arrived, rousing the other cats and getting them excited. They quickly changed their mood, though, as the nurses took us away, one by one. Some mogs were brought back, others weren't. When it came to my turn, my stomach churned with worry about where they were taking me and what was in store for me next.

A feeder carried me into a bright examining room and put me on the table. The V from the previous day looked at me with concern. Thankfully, she didn't have a needle to stab me with, which was what I'd been most scared about. She looked at my lump and prodded it. I couldn't see what she was doing because of the stupid hardhat, but my back stung like an angry wasp. Then she checked over the rest of my body, searching for abnormalities. Desperate for her to take the horrid headpiece off so I could tend to my lump, I cried out, hoping she might understand, but she just smiled at me in that patronising way I'd grown so accustomed to. Once she'd finished her examination, a nurse collected me, returned me to the prison room, and then to the cage. I was strangely glad to be there again. Of course, it wasn't a nice place to be, but it felt a little safer than being carried around, my fate in the hands of the feeders. I licked the rest of the jelly from the food that had been left for me. It was refreshing and nourishing, unlike the solid chunks of unrecognisable gristle underneath. Then I settled in the corner, keeping quiet while the others called out, asking what they'd done to me.

Some time later, the nurse came in and walked straight over to my cell. After opening the door, she attempted to entice me out with a chicken treat. The morsel smelled tasty, but I wasn't going to be tempted so easily. I had no desire to be prodded again, or taken to the examining room for more experiments. But she reached in and grabbed me, and I was in too much discomfort to argue. As she lifted me towards her, my skin stretched down my back, pulling taut across my lump. It felt like my flesh was about to rip open, and it paralysed me, preventing me from defending myself or gripping onto the cage door as she hauled me through it. My lump stung, as if my own precious growth was biting me. As soon as the nurse's shoulder came within reach, I clung on for fear of being dropped and landing on my back. She bent down to the ground and tried to put me into another cage, asking me to walk into it, as if I might want to! But it had a familiar scent and reminded me of home. It was my carrier!

I'd never been grateful to be inside that plastic crate before, but for once, it felt safe. The familiarity was comforting, even though I still had no idea what was coming next or where I'd be going. Was I being taken for another examination? Had Amy arrived to rescue me? Was I about to be adopted by yet another family? The momentary relief at being carried out of the noisy prison room was countered by the anxiety of what my next twist of fate would be.

Seconds later, a door opened, and I recognised my surroundings as the reception area, where the awful nightmare had started. I'd been preparing myself to be carried back to the white room for more probing, poking, and jabbing. Then, in amongst the various voices around me, I heard a familiar tone saying my name. It was Amy! She had come to my rescue, after all. My carrier passed across the counter, and her scent wafted in through the grill door. Sitting silent and scared, I listened to her talking to the nurse. I didn't want to get my hopes up, in case she didn't actually take me home. But she did. She put me in the car that I'd always hated being in, and then not long afterwards, we were in our house and I curled up on her lap, and all was well with the world again.

13. CAT HAT

'Fleas are a cat's greatest nemesis. If your feeder doesn't deal with them, infest the house until they do.' - Mummacat

I was anxious for Amy or Dean to remove my horrid headpiece, but they didn't. Maybe they thought it was some sort of feline fashion statement that I'd chosen to wear, although surely they couldn't have been that stupid. At least the hardhat didn't interfere with my view, since things only came into focus when they were up close. It muffled out sounds, though, so I couldn't pinpoint where noises came from and I'd lose track of where I was.

My beloved lump itched like a flea party. I badly wanted to wash it and find out what the vet had done, but the stupid hat blocked my access and made my regular grooming nigh on impossible.

Walking around the house proved extra challenging because my scentsors were blocked by the solid barrier. I had to use the headpiece like one big whisker, and it was far from efficient. The restraint banged off walls and clattered into furniture, giving me a shock quite different from the usual knocks to the head. I was used to those - my skull would hurt a bit, but I'd pretend it didn't, and after a little lie down I'd be fine again. The horrid headpiece got in the way of pretty much everything. Apart from sleeping, when it made a handy pillow.

I found I could push the hat off over my head if I scratched at it enough and batted it a certain way with my paw, but either Dean or Amy were usually watching, ready to shove it back on. Why they weren't letting me clean myself any more was beyond me. I felt grubby and needed to groom, and it wasn't as if they were attempting to do it for me. More than anything, I needed to scratch my itch and preen my coat.

The hardhat also prevented me from eating properly. Amy at least had the sense to take it off for me to do that, although she put it on again straight afterwards. On the third day, she finally realised I needed to wash after my meal, so she held off on forcing the headpiece back on. That allowed me to regain a little dignity, so I set to work on the mammoth task of playing catch-up on my grooming.

My regime was regular and meticulous, so I was all out of sorts, having been unable to access most of my body for several days. Delighted for the opportunity, I started by washing my paws and legs. Then I worked up my left side, methodically removing hair I no longer had use for, and cleansing away days-old dirt. Keen to get to my lump, which, by that point, itched as if the flea rave had descended into a full-on riot, I gradually edged upwards, towards my spine.

Amy shifted in her seat, watching me carefully, as I licked closer to my growth. I diverted my attention to my tail for a minute and she backed off again. I really couldn't understand what was going on - why my back felt so uncomfortable, and why the feeders wouldn't let me fix it. Amy kept saying 'I can't let you touch it,' and 'it will heal in a few days,' but to me it was obvious I was the only one capable of repairing it.

I decided that the V must have sucked the life out of my poor lump, and put the horrid barrier in place to prevent me from nurturing it back into being. They must have realised I was growing a whole new appendage, and wanted to thwart my plans for fear of the feline species developing into an even more powerful breed. Maybe that's what they thought Missy's cancer was. I felt very lucky they had only tried to destroy my lump, rather than getting rid of me altogether. Something told me I had Amy to thank for that.

As I washed after dinner, I waited until my feeders were looking the other way, and then altered my position and reached my head around. Expecting my growth to resemble a damp, matted mess of deflated fur, what I actually found was far more disturbing. Instead of a saggy coat, I discovered a large bald patch. The V had removed my fur! Why had they thought my lovely coat was causing the problem? No wonder they didn't want me seeing it.

As I licked over the area, anticipating finding some semblance of my precious lump, my tongue caught the corner of something hard and sharp instead. A foreign object seemed to be gripping onto my skin. I grabbed the end of it with my teeth and tugged at it to get it off, but it stung and made the itching worse. The thing on my back was attacking me! I returned fire; biting it and trying to pull it away. It seemed to be some kind of tick that had buried itself into my flesh. My nose and mouth filled with the scent of an open wound. The vile parasite had eaten away my growth! As I reeled in shock, Amy pushed my face away and thrust the hardhat over my head. In an attempt to calm me down, she rubbed my fur and talked to me, but I was too angry to be pacified.

'What on earth is that?!' I cried, 'and why won't you let me remove it? It's itching SO BADLY!' Amy continued trying to appease me, but then she said I might do myself more damage. As if I wasn't the best judge of how to look after my own body! As much as I objected and hopped around, attempting to dislodge the strange giant tick, I had to accept that Amy wasn't going to allow me to scratch the itch or wash my own wound. She was more vigilant after that, only letting me clean my legs and belly before putting the horrid headpiece back on. There were times when the discomfort eased, and moments when the itch was all-consuming. The restraint left me utterly helpless to relieve it, so I had to use all my will power to ride it out.

Despite being physically compromised by the stupid hat, Amy and Dean still expected me to function in the same way I did before. In my opinion, they should at least have carried me to the places I needed to go. They knew my whiskers were incapacitated, but instead of helping me, I heard them laughing as I struggled along the hallway. Going up the stairs was the worst. The bottom of the headpiece would catch on the next step as I reached up, no matter how high I raised my chin. But I was determined, and still fiercely independent. Nothing had stopped me from achieving my goals before, and I wasn't about to let a piece of plastic hold me back. Perhaps the feeders wanted me to fail and flounder, in which case I was going to prove them wrong.

At the end of the week, Amy went away, saying she was going to visit her dad. Although slightly disgruntled, I was glad she didn't take me with her. Another traumatic car journey, after my stressful week, would have been too much. Plus, even though I'd overthrown the hellcats before I left, my horrid hardhat weakened my powers, so Sparkle might have been able to fight back. I could just imagine hearing her whispered taunts seeping up through the floor.

So, it was just me and Dean for a few days. Which was fine. He'd never been a great conversationalist, although he'd become even less talkative than before. Our chats were much shorter and restricted to the necessities; mostly food provisions, and his refusal to remove the stupid hat at any other times. However, he didn't watch me as closely as Amy did, and so I took an opportunity to slip the headpiece off while he was looking the other way. Oh, it felt so satisfying! Finally getting to lick my poor wound and extract that nasty tick. But the more I pulled at it, the more the parasite bit back, and my flesh itched more than ever before, so I had to scratch at it really hard. It wasn't like any insect I'd seen before - and I'd come across my fair share of bugs. Its legs were long and wiry and tough. Too tough to bite through, so I had to rip the beast out, even though it was gripping on deep under my skin.

The tick wasn't giving up the fight, but I couldn't bear the pain any more. I just wanted it to stop, and I knew the only way was to remove the parasite. I got ever so close to defeating the ghastly thing when Dean walked into the room. He swore and panicked, ran over to me and pushed the hardhat over my head. I was furious. I shouted at him to leave me alone, that I needed to finish the job. He replied that I shouldn't have touched it and that the wound looked really bad. What had he expected? If I didn't get rid of the nasty tick, it was hardly likely to step out of its own accord. I paced around, trying to ease the agony, lamenting the fact that I'd been rendered completely helpless to do anything. What cruelty to leave a creature unable to even lick her own wound!

A thought occurred to me, that perhaps the V had put the tick in my back to eat away my new super power and get rid of it once and for all, like I'd seen leeches do on the picture box. On the other hand, the tick might have been there since before my lump had started growing. Maybe that was why my growth had been so persistent and kept coming back after being deflated. And the V burst the growth to get the parasite out, only their plan hadn't worked. So they were leaving the thing there, hoping it would come out on its own one day, or else nibble away at me until I died!

Dean was talking. Not to me, but seemingly to himself, although then I thought I heard Amy's voice, somewhere very far away. Then he put me in the carrier. The pain and shock prevented me from arguing with him. The next thing I knew, I was at the V again, being rushed straight through to one of the white rooms. I felt utterly confused. Had the V planted the tick under my skin? Or had they tried to remove it? There was no time to deliberate over whether or not it was a good place to be. Before I could get my thoughts in order, the V had stabbed me with a needle. The pain stopped, and I went out like a light.

....

When I woke up, I was in prison once again. I just wanted to cry, but I didn't have the energy. Shortly afterwards, a V came to look at me and said I'd be going home soon. I didn't know what 'soon' meant coming from her. It seemed to mean different things to different feeders. However, not long later, I was being ushered into my carrier and handed over to Dean, who took me home. After a deep snooze, my back felt much better than before. The pain had almost gone, and the flea party moved out. Dean gave me lots of cuddles and head scratches that evening, and some chicken treats once my appetite returned. The horrid headpiece was still in place, so I couldn't clean myself, but the day had been so long, I was too exhausted to be angry. Dean must have felt sorry for me, because he let me recharge on his lap for the first time in ages. He'd grown some fat on his belly since the last time, so he wasn't even able to tense his muscles to stop me from making the padding more comfortable.

A couple of days later, Amy came home, and I was so overjoyed to see her, I didn't get upset with her for having been away. I told her all about my traumatic experience and she seemed to understand me, because she said all the right things. After dinner, she left the hardhat off long enough for me to have a good preen. I removed lots of old fur and even checked out what was left of the tick. I was scared about what I'd find, but it turned out the V had extracted most of it. My fur was growing again and the remains of the parasite had given up eating my flesh. The area still itched, but more like a butterfly walking along it than a group of hungry fleas at a buffet. After a few more days, Amy removed the stupid headpiece, and didn't put it back on me again. I could finally clean myself properly, scratch my itches, hear everything normally, and walk around using all my whiskers. It was bliss.

....

That winter, the weather turned colder than ever before, and snow fell for the second time. Throughout the year, the temperature had been a little milder than at Sandbank Crescent, but it was almost as changeable, and the freezing white fluff stayed for longer. I had no desire to go outside, but indoors wasn't much warmer. I'd snuggle up to Amy and use her body heat at night, but I also appreciated the feeder way of sleeping, with a layer on top to keep the heat in. Even a light sheet over me had always felt uncomfortable before. I had fur for a reason, and I didn't want to be weighed down or restricted by anything else. The caves Amy sometimes made under the duvet were cosy nooks, but she'd only hold them open for so long before collapsing them again. I needed space to breathe and move, so blanket-diving wasn't for me.

Feeders aren't clever enough to utilise the thermal benefits of fur. Sometimes they grow hair, but then they remove it and wear extra layers instead. For some reason, it's good enough to keep their heads warm, but not the rest of their bodies. For a species with bigger brains than us, they don't seem to engage them.

Even in the freezing weather, Dean stayed out for longer than he spent at home. I guess he'd found somewhere warmer to be. When he did come back, he reeked of alcohol, and he often slept on the sofa. He and Amy talked less and less, but when they did, they ended up arguing and Amy frequently went to bed upset. When spring finally arrived, the atmosphere in the house grew as cold as the bitter winter had been. Then Amy decided it wasn't good for us to live there anymore. It was time to move again.

14. LONDON

'A truly trustworthy feeder is worth all the milk in the land.' - Mummacat

Amy loaded her belongings into a van, like she had each time before. Packing was a little easier than it had been when we'd moved from Sandbank Crescent, because she left most of the furniture behind with Dean. Even so, I could tell it was harder on her, emotionally. I'd heard her talking to Dean about splitting up their DVD collection and, for some reason, that made her really sad.

The van took us to a place called London. Amy gave me some medicine before we left, squirting it into my mouth. It tasted sweet and came with a chicken treat, so I didn't mind. The journey passed in a sleepy haze.

Our next home was an upstairs flat with a new feeder called Paul. He had his own bedroom, which made me happy, as it meant I didn't have to share my half of the bed with him. Over time, I'd grown used to Amy's accent, but gradually most feeders ended up sounding the same. Paul was different, though. His voice wasn't like Doug's, or Craig's, or Dean's. It had a soft, melodic lilt, apparently due to him coming from somewhere called Belfast.

The flat felt light and airy, and it was easy to find my way around, being all on one level. The floors were polished wood, so I had to walk carefully with my claws primed to keep me from sliding about. But the layout was simple and the space comfortable, so we settled in quickly.

London felt different from Colchester. The air had a slightly denser, grittier quality to it than I was used to; tinged with the aroma of greasy fried chicken. Normally, that would have made me hungry, but it was less alluring when combined with molecules of exhaust fumes, chemicals, and bin juice. Sometimes the ability to pick up on smells from two miles around was regrettable when the breeze wafted in the wrong direction.

The flat had a strange sort of garden, accessed through the living room. There was no cat flap in the door, so I only ventured out when Paul or Amy left it open. Outside, the ground was covered in loose stones and I was dismayed to find no grass or plants to roll about in or chew. A fence ran along two sides, but a gap lead out to a much bigger area. That part had a different kind of floor, like a road surface, only with no cars to sit under. I missed cars. I hadn't seen any since Sandbank Crescent, although I'd heard them from time to time, so I knew they still existed.

The outdoors there was spacious, but didn't have much in it; just a brick wall at each edge, and a big square wooden construction in the middle that rose up out of the ground. The curious structure vibrated from somewhere deep inside, emitting a low whirring noise, like the distant purr of the underworld. Apart from that, the territory was eerily quiet. There was no birdsong, or thrum of car engines, despite the scent of them in the air. I didn't mind, though. I was happy enough wandering about and stretching out on the floor.

One day, I bumped into a set of steps I hadn't noticed before. Deciding they must have been new, I duly went to investigate. Although not smelling recently installed, they also didn't have a well-used aroma, so they clearly warranted an inspection. At the top, I discovered a metal railing, with bars spaced far enough apart for me to slide straight through. Beyond them, a long, narrow pathway curved up around my feet. The surface felt like no alleyway or footpath I'd ever walked before, so I was eager to find out where it lead to. Would there be a whole new garden to explore? Fresh territory, with birds I could hunt, or a cosy nook I could sleep in, perhaps? Padding along the strange path, excited at the prospect of making a groundbreaking discovery, I arrived at a solid brick wall. My whiskers couldn't find a way over it or past it, and the funny footpath ended abruptly, so there was no route to the right or left. Aromas of rotting leaves and dried, stagnant water drifted up from beneath my paws. It was time to return home.

As I made to turn around, I realised the space I stood in was narrower than me. Almost too tight to switch direction. Thankfully, I was able to utilise some yoga moves to snake myself back around, but then all I had ahead of me was more of the same pathway. Then I wasn't sure which way I was facing, and I had no point of reference for where the stairs were that had brought me there in the first place.

I had no idea what was beyond the edge of the curved path, but when I reached out a paw, the air was empty. Tentatively stepping over the side, I expected to find solid ground, but there was nothing there. Then I caught a breath of wind and realised it smelled cleaner and thinner, as if I was looking out of a high window. I called out, but my cries didn't rebound off any walls or echo into a room, the sound just vanished into the atmosphere. The sensation of being suspended up above the floor, with no way down, made me wobbly on my paws. I kept shouting, hoping Amy would respond. She wasn't normally very far away, but I couldn't hear her or smell her. I cried out louder, my throat straining, but then I started feeling dizzy and light-headed. Too scared to move, I managed to hold my balance by focussing on my pads' connection with the footpath.

Finally, floating through the silence, I caught a distant echo of Amy calling out to me. I shouted in response, and a few moments later, the sound of her footsteps filled me with joy. She was getting closer. At one point, she sounded only a few tails away. But then her voice drifted past me and disappeared off in another direction. She hadn't seen me. She didn't know where I was. Had I vanished out of sight? Was I as invisible to her as everything else now was to me? She sounded lost, wandering around and saying my name. I called her back, but she couldn't find me. Then her footsteps grew louder again, and her voice sounded closer. Much closer. She must have been walking up the steps that I had gone up before finding myself on the pathway. Thank goodness, she'd almost reached me!

'Molly, there you are!' Her words were the best words I'd ever heard. Amy had come to save me, as I knew she would. 'What are you doing up there, in the gutter? Come on, come here.' Still standing on the curved path, with no idea how to get back, I waited to feel her hands wrap around me and lift me to safety. Instead, she kept calling to me, instructing me to go to her. There were two or three tails between us, and Amy wasn't moving. I was on a tightrope, scared to put a paw wrong in case I fell to my death, or paralysis. I tentatively lifted one paw, then another, creeping forwards, following the direction of her voice. After a few steps, I could smell her scent, and when her fingers touched my head, relief flooded through me like a tidal wave. Elated to be saved, I stopped. I waited for her to pick me up, but she continued saying my name and asked me to keep going. Why wasn't she ending my horrific ordeal? I demanded she come and rescue me before something terrible happened, but she stubbornly stayed where she was, calling to me more persistently. So I took another careful step forward, and then another, and then her hands slid down my shoulders and lifted me up into her sturdy embrace. I was safe! Amy carried me back indoors, and I curled up on the sofa, and everything was alright again.

I didn't go back near those stairs after that. The thought of what was up there and the memory of getting stuck kept me firmly on ground level. Outdoors was still fun to explore though, and I even made some new feeder friends there once. After chatting for a while, they petted me and gave me tuna and asked me lots of questions. My mouth was too busy to answer them, but they wouldn't have understood my explanation, anyway. Why do feeders do that? They ask cats questions, knowing full well they won't know what we're saying in reply. It's a shame they can't understand meowlings, they'd learn a lot.

....

Paul wasn't around much. A few times a week he'd arrive home late, smelling of alcohol, but not in the same way Dean used to.

I'd know how inebriated Paul was by the length of time his key rattled against the lock before it opened, and the pattern of his unsteady footsteps pacing down the hall. He'd chat to me in his sing-song voice, which became proportionately more tuneful with the strength of his boozy breath. He also brought home tasty treats when he'd been out drinking, half of which invariably ended up abandoned, uneaten, on the kitchen counter. After regaling me with his exploits from his evening out, he'd warn me not to jump up to eat his leftover chicken. So, once he'd gone to bed, that's exactly what I did, obviously.

Paul seemed like a trustworthy feeder, and Amy clearly thought so too, so I took to re-energising on his lap when he was in and she was out. Often, he'd make football appear in the picture box. Amy never watched sports. I'd heard her say she wasn't a fan. Craig used to love football, but I mostly ignored it. However, since Paul spent most evenings watching the 'the beautiful game' as he called it, and shouting for Man Yoo, I slowly started to take an interest. Once I'd learned to understand the commentary, I found myself getting excited as the tiny players batted their ball across the grass. As fun a pastime as it was, Paul took it ever so seriously, and the level of attention he paid me would vary greatly, depending on the final score.

One quiet day when the feeders were out, I came across a ball in the flat. It had rolled out from under the sofa when Paul pushed the vacuum machine that sucked up my old fur. The small toy jangled along the floor, which I'd never heard the one in the picture box do. But I was inspired, so I tapped it with my paw and it tinkled off to the other side of the room. I followed after it, and then kicked it somewhere else, using the table legs for goal posts. The ball ricocheted off walls and furniture, and I chased it around until my energy ran out and I stopped for a nap.

Amy didn't judge my behaviour, and I rarely worried about what she thought of my activities; on the contrary, I needed her on board for my walks. However, I was aware of her distaste for football, so out of respect, I resisted playing it when she was in the room. The last thing I wanted to do was upset her, since I relied on her to open the back door for me every day. Once or twice, she found the ball while tidying up, but I feigned disinterest and pretended I knew nothing about it.

Since she didn't see me playing, she must have thought I was missing out, so she brought in a new plush victim for me to practice my hunting on. I had enough exercise from the football, but to cover my tracks and avoid Amy's suspicion, I enthusiastically fought with the new predator. To be fair, it was the perfect size for me to roll around the floor with and cuddle as I kicked and bit it, trying out a new 'draw them in with kindness, then stab them in the back' technique. If I had any future Hellcat battles, I'd be ready.

I had a few new opportunities to hunt while in that flat. Early on, a large family of cockroaches moved in, and I did my best to deal with the invasion. I batted a few of them out of the kitchen, sending them scuttling off under the cupboards, but they raced away faster than my eyes could see, so killing them proved tricky. Word must have spread through their verminous network that I was hunting them down, because after a few days, they stayed away and never returned.

Another time, when Amy was away, some mice had the audacity to come into the flat, looking for food. Paul missed a massacre while he was out at Work. I slaughtered and consumed so many tiny rodents that, by the time he got back, my stomach couldn't contemplate another one. They kept coming in, but I'd done my part, and it was Paul's turn to take up the mantle. Instead of culling them himself, he got mechanical traps to do the deed, and then gloated that he'd dealt with the problem. At one point, he picked me up and put me near a squirming victim, but having disposed of so many myself already, I left him the pleasure of cleaning up the rest.

....

The days grew darker, the temperature dropped, and the snow came again. The flat was much warmer than the previous house had been, so I took my exercise indoors, free from the discomfort of the cold. Our bedroom had a large space of clear floor, which I used to pace around, with the security of knowing I wouldn't bump into anything. In my mind, I explored uncharted lands, hunting out sky birds and following trails never trodden before by feline-kind. All sorts of adventures played out in my head during those imaginary hikes. I could go anywhere and do anything without the risk of ending up lost or injured. I chased tuna in great rivers without getting wet. I scaled mountains and found giant tweeters, like the ones Craig used to get the feathers from, and I'd hunt them down and kill them for dinner. I walked through forests and climbed trees and invented whole new worlds to explore and sniff. The possibilities were endless. And then, when I'd had enough of walking, I'd stop, and find myself back in the safety of home, with Amy, and the bed, and the sofa, and my food dish.

Amy spent a lot of time out of the flat. She didn't have a regular daily schedule, so she came and went at different times, often going to Work in the mornings, but occasionally setting off later in the day. Don't get me wrong, I was content with entertaining myself, but I was always happiest when she was there for company. Since she wasn't always home at mealtimes, she swapped my food bowl for a fancy device that opened by itself. Before she went out, she would fill it with food, teasing me by opening packets but then trapping the treats under a plastic lid so I couldn't get to them. No amount of pawing at the robotic feeder, or flashing it my pleading eyes persuaded it open early, no matter how hungry I was. Although I always preferred to take my meals when Amy was there, and my appetite normally disappeared when I was lonely. So when the machine did release the food, I would often ignore its whirring declaration of dinner time, putting myself on hunger strike until Amy was back home.

When she was there, her lap was the warmest, comfiest spot, and the way she gently rubbed my fur soothed my senses, such that I'd purr for hours. She treated me with loving affection, and fussed me whenever I wanted (and sometimes when I didn't), and it made me feel cherished, even in her absence. Of course, I had to put up with her odd ways, but then us animals always see the strangest sides of feeders, that they wouldn't dare show anyone else. Felines are intuitive, so we know what our feeders need, but we're also entirely accepting of their quirky behaviours. Feeders find us comforting and grounding, which makes us a positive influence on their mental health. A large part of that is down to them allowing themselves to be honest around us, with no falseness or embarrassment. I've seen feeders on their own and with others. Mostly, when it's just me and them, they're relaxed and genuine, but when another member of their own species is in the room, they put on a mask; surrounding themselves with an air of modesty, as if they've sprayed themselves with a scent of decency. Us cats know what's underneath. We see the ugly side, the truthful side, and we accept them as they are. Feeders can be their authentic selves around animals, and that's what makes us good for their psyches. Now, if they would only listen to our advice, they really could be the superior species!

15. CATTITUDE

'If you can see past your vision and watch from your soul, you will be wiser than any creature on earth.' - Mummacat

Half way through our stay in the flat, Paul moved out, and a girl called Lottie moved in. Where Paul had been warm and fun, Lottie was cooler and more serious. She didn't laugh as much, and when she did, it was more of a tight, reserved giggle than Paul's carefree belly laugh. She was friendly enough, but mostly stayed in her bedroom. After a few weeks, we met her boyfriend, Toby. He usually visited late in the evenings, because he was an entrepreneur. Apparently, that meant his parents had lots of money that he used to start an online business in Shoreditch with his friend Rupert, and it took up all of his time. Toby was a very fussy eater who covered every meal in red, gloopy ketchup.

Amy had a new man in her life, too, called Joe, who visited the flat once a week or so. Always very cheerful, he lavished me with attention, but I could tell it was mostly for show. Joe's happiness was surface-deep. In his world, every day glowed with sunshine and rainbows, but rainbows rarely exist without grey clouds, and his lurked beneath his shiny facade. Amy was besotted with him, and her happiness was infectious, but I could see dark times ahead. My aptitude for reading feeder's truths revealed that at some point Joe would break her heart. But that would come later.

Amy got a new job and told me she had to go away again for a while, like she used to. I overheard her talking to Lottie about it and asking her to look after me in her absence. The arrangement didn't sound appealing. Lottie wasn't the best company. She was another one who pretended to be a feline ally, but she only bonded with particular cats, and I wasn't on the list. Amy hadn't yet decided if she trusted Lottie enough to care for me, but she was hoping to get reassurance from her before the time came. So, I spent the following few weeks being as annoying as I could when Amy was out, to make Lottie like me even less. I cried while she cooked in the kitchen, and when she ate dinner, I interrupted and tried to steal her food. Reluctant to share her spoils with me, she occasionally gave in and threw me the odd paltry scrap in an attempt to shut me up. When she hid away in her bedroom, I stationed myself outside her door and shouted. I jumped on her lap whenever she sat down. I sat on Toby too, at every opportunity, which annoyed him, because my fur coated his work clothes. It seemed like a big fuss to me, considering they were only jeans and t-shirts. Once or twice, I pooped outside my toilet box, so Lottie had to clean it up, but she just left it there and Amy tidied it away when she got home instead. One evening, as Lottie and Toby relaxed on the sofa watching a romantic film, I found the remote control on the floor and trod on the buttons to change the channel, just as it got to a good bit.

As Mission Annoy Lottie progressed nicely, Amy threw another spanner in the works. She brought home a feeder called Gary and said he'd be staying in her room while she was away. Gary seemed like a very shady character to me - all charm and bravado - but I didn't buy it. He had a hint of the Nip about him, but not the kind that I liked. Why Amy had brought him home was beyond me, but I worried that if two feeders were going to be in the flat, Amy would consider that a suitable solution for my care. Was she going to leave me there with a pair of virtual strangers while she disappeared to goodness-knows-where, for goodness knows how long? Surely she knew I wouldn't put up with that.

Every day, I hoped to hear that Amy's Work had fallen through, but no such news arrived. Then I overheard Lottie saying she wasn't going to be home enough to help with cat-sitting duties after all. My plan had worked! She was making excuses to avoid looking after me. That just left Gary, and I knew Amy wouldn't leave me with only a dubious stranger for company. Surely with Lottie withdrawing her offer, Amy had to cancel her Work and stay at home with me instead. As it transpired, I was partially right, although the outcome wasn't exactly what I'd hoped for. Despite claiming to be anxious about leaving me, she didn't cancel her trip. However, instead of me flat-sharing with smarmy Gary and aloof Lottie, I was to go and board with her mum.

Once I knew for sure that Amy wasn't prepared to give up her Work for me, I realised I'd been at risk of being taken to a cattery. The thought of going to her mum's put my nerves on edge, but still I thanked the great Bastet, for saving me a more terrible fate. Amy had never talked about sending me to cat prison, but then my first family didn't prepare me for it either. When we lived in Sandbank Crescent, Amy and Craig went away for two weeks, and a man called Tam moved in while they were gone. Tam had visited us before, so I knew he was a genuine ally. He was friendly and easy-going, and I'd warmed to him instantly. During our fortnight together, he mostly watched the picture box and drank from cans. The liquid smelled fruity, but not in a nice way, so I didn't partake. Every day, he delivered my meals in a timely fashion, gave me treats, took me for walks, and treated me with the respect all felines deserve from their feeders. Each time Amy disappeared for Work, she made sure a responsible provider was there to fulfil my needs, so I had no doubt she would always look for the best option when it came to my wellbeing.

The following week, Amy scooped me up into my carrier and walked me down the road to the V. For a minute, I was concerned that 'staying at Mum's' was actually code for cat prison. The white-coated feeder prodded and poked me, but thankfully didn't carry me off and put me into a cell. Amy proved her trustworthiness once again and took me back home. As she packed for her trip and tidied up her room ready for Gary to stay in it, I pondered on the odd arrangement. The room could look after itself for a few months, and Lottie certainly didn't need the company. Still, Amy seemed to think it was a good idea.

On the day we left, Amy's mum arrived to collect us. Amy gave me a mouthful of the medicine I'd had before the last time we'd moved, so I don't remember much of the journey. Her mum had come to visit several times over the years, so I knew her to be friendly and kind. Her voice sounded like Amy's, so her tone was reassuringly familiar. In Amy's absence, she was probably the next best feeder to spend my time with. When we arrived at the house, I met Steve. He also lived there, but mostly avoided me throughout my stay. Apparently, he was allergic, whatever that meant. I sensed that he thought I might jump up and bite him at any moment, so I generally left him alone. Soon after I arrived, I heard him call Amy's mum Ros, so I guessed that was the name she went by.

Ros and Steve's home was in a place called Farnham, which must have been out in the countryside, because the air smelled fresher than I'd breathed in years. Free of exhaust fumes and aromas of greasy food and chemicals, the oxygen glided through my airways as smoothly as fresh cream slipped down my throat. Overall, it felt like a much healthier place to be. The first thing I did, once released from my carrier, was orientate myself. The house was large and comfortable, and as I explored the hallway, I overheard Ros telling Amy she didn't want me going upstairs. Naturally, that piqued my curiosity, and I climbed the stairs immediately. Once I'd investigated the first floor, I had no reason to venture up there again, apart from when the feeders were out and I needed to do my safety checks. Besides, there was enough space downstairs, and I found plenty of cushions to make into beds. I especially liked the ones on top of the sofas, where I could take my rightful position above the feeders, and where the late sun shone through the window and gently warmed my coat.

Different feeders came to the house during my stay, and they all loved talking about me. In the mornings, they sat around a big table, eating breakfast and cooing over my appearance. 'Cute' was a word I heard often throughout my life, and it was a quality that compelled feeders to pet me. I'll admit, I made the most of opportunities afforded me on the premise that I was 'cute'. Even back at Doug's, he gave up kicking me off the furniture because I had an adorable face. What Mummacat taught had me as a kitten had worked out just as she said it would. By switching my expression from demanding to imploring, Doug soon gave in and let me stay on the sofa, or allow me to rest on his lap. This method came in handy for endearing myself to feeders ever since, and it served me well. At the breakfast table in Farnham, I received scraps of sausage and bacon once Ros left the room. And when she came back, she told her guests how good-natured and sweet I was.

Once I'd settled into the house, Ros let me out to the garden on crisp, dry days. Crunchy brown leaves carpeted the green lawn, and bright flowers adorned the borders. Various birds dappled the sky, swooshing in and out of trees. In stark contrast to the sparse terrace at the London flat, the outdoors there contained all the things I had missed for a long time. The twitter of birds up above was a welcome sound, but I could barely see them as they darted through the air, almost completely fuzzed out like everything else. I didn't mind too much. I still had my whiskers and my scentsors, as well as my acute hearing, which I tuned in and out through the day.

On one occasion, I nearly got lost outdoors. I crawled through a bush to investigate what was on the other side, and found more grass, flower beds, and plants to sniff. I caught an unfamiliar smell lingering in the air, and realised I'd entered into another territory. I turned to go back through to Ros' garden, but the hole in the hedge had vanished. Poking my whiskers into the damp undergrowth was futile, as the dense tangle of branches seemed impenetrable. My heart beat faster as I struggled to find a gap big enough to squeeze through. Then I heard Ros calling out my name. Following the direction of her familiar voice, I made my way back along the hedge wall. Once I got close to her calls, I tried again to cut through the leaves. Thankfully, they gave way, and moments later, Ros' fingers grazed the top of my head. I clambered through the bush towards her, and broke out the other side, walking straight into her legs. She sounded really pleased to see me, saying something about not wanting to have to tell Amy she'd lost me. But I was too busy purring and winding around her ankles in gratitude to take it in. From then on, I made sure I stayed the right side of the bushes, and took to my imaginary exploring indoors. The sitting room floor was big enough for me to pace a circle in, so I walked and walked, imagining I was deep in an ancient wood, or a field of long grass, or back in the flat with Amy and all our things.

Ros was efficient with my mealtime schedule, and she and Steve got up earlier than me most mornings, which Amy never had. Life there was peaceful, especially as there weren't any other animals nearby to bother me. However, the more time passed, the more I worried that Amy might never come back. I began to feel anxious and lonely. Ros was lovely, but she kept busy around the house, and went out shopping, and, well, she wasn't Amy. I was used to Amy. The bond we'd developed ran deep, and she understood me like no other feeder could. Plus, I liked the way she scritched behind my ears. She knew just the right angle to rub my jawbone and the perfect pressure to massage my paws. I'm not too proud to admit I pined for her. Occasionally she came to visit, but not often, and never for long. Every time she did, it was wonderful to spend even a short while in her company. On most occasions, I happened to be taking a nap when she arrived. Her voice softly whispered my name, filtering into my sleep as though she were part of my dream - which she frequently was anyway - but then I'd wake up and she would really be there, like my dream had come true! She'd stay a while, either for a couple of hours, or overnight, and then disappear again.

16. REUNITED

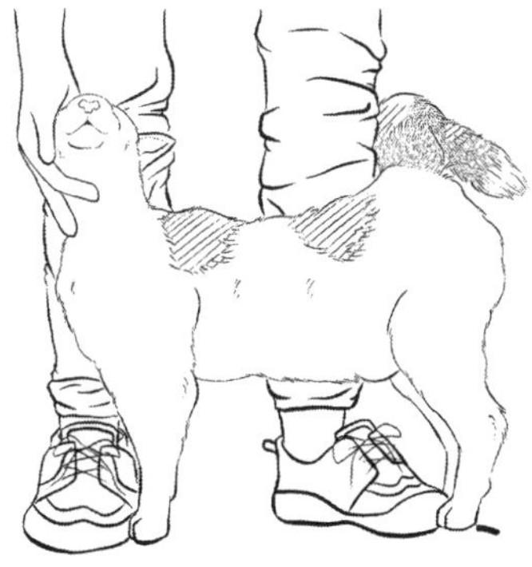

'The right *feeder* is worth making compromises *for.*' - Mummacat

The weather turned colder, and the days grew darker. Although the atmosphere in the house was warm, the gradual unfolding of a gloomy winter reflected my mood. I was out of sorts and restless. Food lost its flavour and lethargy set in. Feeders would have called my affliction 'anxiety and depression'. It affected all my senses.

After many weeks of malaise, Amy returned. With barely a 'hello' she put me in the carrier, placed it into Ros' car, and away we went. Heading home. At last, normality would resume, and I'd soon be comfy in the flat, with Amy, where we belonged. As my daydreams of cosy home life filled my head with happy thoughts, they were rudely interrupted as the car came to an abrupt halt, and I was lifted out. The trip hadn't been long enough for us to be back in London. Amy carried me into a building, where I was instantly confronted by a host of horribly familiar smells. Chemicals, animals, medicine, and strangers. The V. The hope I'd managed to gather with my last remnants of energy dissolved into the bleached surroundings of yet another white examining room.

As it happened, the V treated me as gently and kindly as I could have hoped for. She did the usual prodding and poking and then took me off into a separate room to carry out some experiments on me that no other V had before. She stretched my eyelids open so that everything burned bright, and then turned dark again. Next, she wrapped a wide band around my leg. A clicky whirring sound purred beside me and the cuff expanded, growing bigger and bigger, like the giant peach in the mini-feeder story. Or like a balloon the feeders blow up for birthday parties. Only my leg was in the middle of it. The strange device gripped on so tightly as it swelled up, I thought my limb would be squeezed right off! Thankfully, it stopped short of snapping my bone in two, but I didn't dare move my paw for fear of permanent repercussions. What if the V planned to leave it there forever, and I'd have to live with it? The leg balloon would be even worse than the horrid hardhat! After a minute, the grip loosened and my limb was released intact. What a relief! Why the V needed to test my bone strength, I'll never know.

Once that ordeal was over, she pulled at my mouth to look at my teeth and gums. I half-expected her to force-feed me some medicine under the pretence of a dental check-up, but I was spared that trauma, at least. She said I was a good girl and took me back through to Amy and Ros. Amy cuddled me and said everything was going to be fine, and I told myself to believe her. My faith in her was the only glint I had left of a light at the end of my cold, miserable tunnel. The feeders talked about my health for a while, before concluding the obvious; that my pining for Amy's company was the cause of my depression. Also known as separation anxiety. In the car afterwards, I asked Bastet for one last favour, even though my faith in her had all but disappeared. I prayed our next destination would be London, so things could return to normal, with Amy there every day. But my remaining bubble of trust in the deity deflated like the leg balloon, as the car stopped, my carrier was jolted out, and I found myself back in Ros and Steve's house. Amy disappeared back to Work, and I resumed my spot on the cushion on the sofa, and napped.

Time passed slowly, and I moved through each day shrouded in a heavy fog. I mostly slept and occasionally ate, with very little motivation to do much else. With Amy away, I felt like half my tail was missing. Everything was slightly off balance. Ros continued to look after me with care and affection, doing her best to keep my spirits up, but I couldn't pull my heart out of its gloom.

The next time Amy visited, there was something different about her. She arrived with a renewed energy, as if she had a great secret to tell me. As depleted as I was of all strength and motivation, I managed to climb into her lap and purr with contentment. Then she said the magic words. 'Molly, we're going home.'

Instantly, my mood lifted, the dark clouds finally parting. My grey world brightened and fresh energy flowed through my bones. Ros and Steve had been kind guardians, but Amy was the only feeder I really wanted to be with. So, once again back in my carrier, I couldn't have been happier to be in the car. I wasn't given any medicine before the trip, and adrenaline kept me alert for the entire journey. It wasn't nearly as traumatic as before, though, because I was with Amy, and we were going home!

....

The flat was almost as we'd left it, and it felt like home again in no time. Our bedroom smelled funny for a while, because of Gary and his special Nip, but Amy opened the windows and put fresh sheets on the bed (which I helped with, of course), and soon his stench wore away. The familiar aromas of London filled my scentsors and, although I'd enjoyed the clean air of Farnham, the comfort of my home territory mattered more to me than luxury surroundings. Deep bonds and happy hearts are worth far more than material effects.

Amy and I had a perfect few days, with her being at home most of the time, before she started more Work and disappeared at odd hours again. I always knew she'd come back, though. Occasionally, she stayed away overnight, at Joe's. That was okay with me, because for the most part, she returned glowing with happiness, and it pleased me to see her that way, even though I didn't entirely trust Joe's motives. Before my stay at Ros' house, her feelings for him had started to run deep, but sometimes she came home sad, and I sensed he wasn't treating her as well as she deserved. His emotions were floating on the surface like a colourful slick of oil, whereas Amy's flowed like an undercurrent, holding strong against the tide that should have swept her away. However, since we'd been back in London, they seemed more balanced. Joe was being more attentive and showing signs of commitment, although I remained unconvinced of his genuine desires. A couple of times, I asked him what his intentions were with my feeder, but he hadn't understood, of course. He responded with a patronising pat on the head and an insincere, 'Awww you're so cute.' I wouldn't be won over so easily. Besides, he wasn't telling me anything I didn't already know. Joe was not a pet person, I could tell.

Day to day, life was good, and I enjoyed pottering about at a slightly slower pace. Lottie warmed to me a little more, seeing as I'd ended my harassment campaign against her. When she was home she petted me and even gave me the odd treat.

By that time, the winter had fully broken, and Amy and I snuggled up in the warm flat when she wasn't at Work or out with Joe. Then she started going to a different Work, at a theatre and a school, which she said was more stable but it meant being out for longer every day. As soon as I'd eaten my breakfast, she'd be gone, sometimes not returning until late in the evening. With Lottie often out or shut away in her bedroom, and no-one to fuss me or play games with, I whiled away my days kicking the football around the living room, or snoozing on the bed.

Sleep had always been one of my favourite activities, and as I grew older, slumber became ever more appealing. I spent many hours dreaming of my happiest times with Amy, and running about in fields of grass, chasing colourful butterflies. My heart would sink when I woke to find the flat empty and still, although I'd soon drift off again, eventually roused by Amy coming home, and finding another chunk of time had passed by. The days became shorter and the seasons changed faster, or at least it felt like they did.

Amy told me Work was a long way away, and that's why she had to be out so much. At least it wasn't so far that she felt it necessary to take me to stay at Ros and Steve's. Then, one day, she mentioned moving house again. She wanted to live closer to Work so she wouldn't have to be out for so many hours, and we could spend more time together. I liked the sound of that.

She found another place for us to live and off we went, in a van full of our belongings. With my age catching up with me, moving felt like more stress than my body could handle. But I reminded myself that no cat is too old for a new adventure. I was still agile enough, and had all my brain cells, although my muscles were growing weary and I had less inclination to spend most of my time exploring. The van ride was tiring and stressful. Apparently, the next house was also in London, but given how long the journey took, it might as well have been in Catmandu. As well as Amy and Joe up front with us, her friend Neil came along too, and they all chatted and played music on the way. The aroma of three feeders, plus the plethora of van smells, overwhelmed my scentsors. All sorts of chemicals attacked my nostrils; various fragrances designed to smell nice battling with each other alongside the grease and dirt ground into the carpets and seats. Having grown used to a calmer, quieter life, the sudden sensory overload was almost unbearable.

Amy kept me in my carrier the whole time, refusing me the freedom to survey the environment, or even sit on her lap. I cried out, trying my hardest to use feeder tongue so they might understand. Being confined made me nauseous, and I just wanted to be let out of the box. Amy finally understood my message, but instead of honouring my request, they all laughed at my attempt at their language, and teased me about it. Eventually, we arrived at our new home, and not a moment too soon. All my remaining shreds of regard for Joe had fizzled away, since he clearly didn't respect Amy enough to treat me with a suitable degree of dignity.

As we entered the house, the change in atmosphere was delicious. The air smelled far more acceptable than in the ghastly van, and the atmosphere had a warm, calm vibe about it. The ground was coated in soft carpets instead of the slippery solid wood floors of the flat, and there were stairs again, with other levels to explore. I found plenty of beds to sleep on, and best of all, the house had a garden with grass and sunshine. And Amy was there. She didn't have to spend so long out at Work every day anymore, so we had lots more time together.

As I had predicted, the romance between Amy and Joe turned cold. Their relationship had iced over a few times in the course of the previous months, but she kept going back to him, hoping her warmth would thaw it out. He had charm, I'd give him that, but she was blinded by his sunshine, unable to see the stirring grey clouds underneath. Amy lacked the feline intuition to understand that he wasn't good for her; that he could never give her what she needed, no matter how long she waited. Her higher knowledge had been drowned out as she convinced herself that he was lost at sea and she could help him navigate to safety. And she did, in a way. At her suggestion, Joe sought counselling and discovered a genuine blue sky beyond the depression. Sadly, though, once he'd found himself, his compass took him sailing off in a different direction. I gave her all the comfort I was capable of providing and reassured her that she was still loved, although I couldn't entirely fill the void that remained. That said, a little feline love can make a big difference, being a natural remedy to aid the feeder healing process. Amy was stronger than she knew, but the spell Joe had cast over her was destined to break, and it left her stranded. Of course, I was painfully aware that my leaving would have a far more devastating effect, but we can't choose when that happens. Even I didn't know until it was too late.

17. FURWELL

'When it's time to go, you'll know.' - Mummacat

The morning of my departure was an ordinary one; a peaceful start to a promising, lazy Sunday, although nobody could have predicted what it had in store for me. After a short yoga stretch, followed by a re-charge on Amy's resting hip, I woke her for breakfast at precisely 7a.m. Mummacat had taught me to fill up with a hearty meal before setting off on any new adventure, and although I had no special plans that day, I had adopted her policy to always be prepared.

Amy had arrived home late the previous night and since I hadn't managed to persuade her, in all our years together, that shorter naps were better than long sleeps, she went straight back to bed after serving my food and giving me a good-morning head-rub. I don't think she realised how much her tiny gestures meant to me. Compelled to display her affections in a clear and deliberate fashion, she'd make vocal declarations and grand, fussy acts of kindness. But just the way she ruffled my fur and scritched behind my ears was enough for me to know her true feelings. Likewise, I would lick her chin, or brush up against her face to show my love for her. We were linked, her and me. We had a bond unlike any other, and I'm certain it was deeper than most felines and their feeder's. Frequently, I saw other cats spending their days on solitary outdoor explorations, only returning home to eat and nap, indifferent to their providers until meal times came around. Mummacat had the same attitude; regarding her feeders as simply slaves to her demands. Amy meant so much more to me than that.

Anyway, I digress. After breakfast, I had a good wash by the back door, enjoying the morning sunshine beaming through the glass. It was going to be another glorious, warm day. I pondered the temperature, hoping for a steady rise so Amy and I could spend some time in the garden, which was always her preference when the sun was out. With nothing else doing, I opted for a nap while I waited for her to wake. So, I climbed the stairs to the bedroom, jumped on the bed, and curled up in the crook behind her knees.

As I snoozed, I dreamed with perfect HD vision. Birds flew around my head, lush green grass softly yielded beneath my paws, and fluorescent flowers sprung up everywhere: reds, yellows, pinks and purples patterning the borders. I rolled on the cool lawn, enjoying the sweet, balmy dew, watching the sparrows swooping above. The tweeters darted about, taunting my urge to hunt. Instinctively, I trained my eye on the juiciest: the one that looked as though he'd had more than his fair share of the garden worms. As I primed my claws, ready to leap into an attack, the ground underneath me shook. An earthquake rippled through my body and sucked the air from my lungs. Trying desperately to inhale, I could only manage sharp, shallow gasps as I strained for oxygen. Every muscle in my body froze into a state of paralysis. My desperate efforts to move were usurped by a sensation normally reserved for nightmares; when you're struggling through a dense puddle of mud while being chased by an aggressive, slabbering dog, who's gaining on you by the second. Only that wasn't my dream. I was still lying in the grass, looking up at the cobalt blue sky. A grey cloud drifted past.

The ground rocked again and stole my breath. Once more, I panted through the quake until my muscles relaxed. A muffled noise grazed through from somewhere. It sounded like Amy's comforting tones. I looked across the garden and felt compelled to walk, which, surprisingly, I was able to do. The movement came so easily, and for the first time since the accident, my hip glided smoothly, without clicking. I had no clue where I was going, but something was urging me on, away from the house. Away from Amy.

The moment didn't feel stressful or sad, and I knew she would be okay, even though I was padding away from her. Leaving her. As I walked, a series of vivid colours gradually hazed into view. They were soft and muted to start with, but became brighter the closer I got, separating out and sharpening against each other. Then, right before me, glowing bright in its reflection of the sun, shone a beautiful rainbow. I'd seen one before, in my youth, but I didn't recall it being so striking. This spectacle was vast, filling the entire horizon, and so close now.

I reached the edge, where the spectrum of luminescent shades met the earth and melted into the shimmering green grass. A familiar sensation brushed over my head. It was Amy's hand, gently stroking me, as her voice whispered my name. She was calling me back, but my path was set before me, beckoning me on. There was no turning around. Not this time. Amy didn't realise it, but she was saying goodbye. She didn't need to tell me she loved me. I knew.

ABOUT THE AUTHOR

I have been writing for most of my life, in various forms, although this is the first completed project that has made it to publication (with the exception of 2 poems printed in anthologies half a lifetime ago). Having always loved the idea of writing a book, I only became brave enough to share my work in recent years, discovering it might just be good enough to let loose on the general public.

My love for Molly and my determination to keep her memory alive motivated me to get her memoir written and shared. I've thoroughly enjoyed exploring the world from her perspective, blurring the lines between fact and fiction along the way.

You can find more photos of Molly, and a blog about my writing, at www.soulcat.co.uk

I currently live in Bedford, with my partner, Rob, and dog, Skip.

ABOUT THE PHOTOGRAPHER

Since capturing Molly's natural beauty back in 2004, Craig Aitchison has gone on on to become an award-winning photographer, specialising in panoramic images of the Scottish Highlands.

Craig has spent over twenty-five years walking and exploring in the beauty of Scotland's mountains, glens and lochs. Combining a passion for the wild with an affinity for traditional film photography, he was the inaugural winner of the Scottish Landscape Photographer of the Year.

You can find more of his work at www.landandlight.co.uk

ABOUT THE ILLUSTRATOR

Elly graduated Coventry University with a degree in Fine Art and Illustration, and her freelance illustration business Ellypop Illustration was born. Specialising in quirky brush pen illustrations, character design and typography, Elly's latest works have been doing pet pawtraits!

You can find Elly in the following places:
Instagram: @ellypop
Facebook: facebook.com/EllypopIllustration
Etsy: etsy.com/shop/Ellypop

ACKNOWLEDGEMENTS

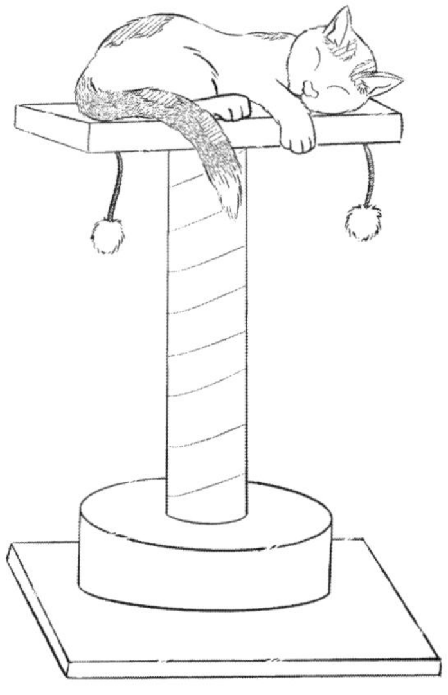

'Never forget, you're always the most important presence in a room.' - Mummacat

This book has been an eight and a half year passion project I wasn't sure I'd ever see come to life outside my head, my notebook and my MacBook. My words have been drafted, re-drafted, edited and shelved. Then re-written, re-edited, augmented, a whole new perspective explored, and then moulded into what you have in your hands today.

I have so many people to thank for helping me bring this book to fruition. My deepest gratitude goes to my biggest cheerleader, Rob Reddan, who believed in my writing and gave me the encouragement I needed to get it done. My brilliant team of beta readers all contributed valuable feedback through my various drafts, and motivated me to put Molly's story out into the world. Lucy Joan Barnes, whose lockdown book club has been invaluable in so many ways, and along with the other members; Sabrina Gonzalez-Sammut, Emma Joy-Staines and Louise Norton, gave me enormous encouragement and useful notes. I also received wonderful feedback from Jennie P Sinclair, who I connected with through Writer's HQ (whose no-nonsense courses, motivating newsletters and incredibly helpful & encouraging community are a writer's dream). Thanks also to Kevin Spurgeon at Dignity pet crematorium, who gave me invaluable insider information about his industry.

They say you should never ask your mum what she thinks of your work, because she'll be too biased to be honest. I'm lucky that mine - Ros Knowles - is a grammar superstar, and she's been an immense help with this book - not least for the random phone calls asking for grammar advice! I am also proud to credit her with some of the creative input, including the term 'feeders'. My brother, Tim Vaughan-Spencer has also been invaluable, becoming a last-minute editor and helping with the blurb. My dad, Simon Vaughan-Spencer provided encouragement, all-important biased praise, and approval to write about his mother in a less than flattering light.

Thanks to Craig Aitchison, for his stunning photography, as seen on the front cover and in most of the Part 1 chapters. A few were taken by me, but it's been too long to remember! Elly Hudson's beautiful illustrations brought Molly's own story to life. Her immense patience through many edits and revisions of her brilliant work was spectacular. At one point I was convinced she must have created a voodoo doll with my name on it, but she was professional and wonderful throughout the process, and the results meow for themselves.

As a final note, I would like to thank all the people who were a part of mine and Molly's journey; some named and some not. Craig Aitchison, Colin Marshall, Paul Quinn (who I re-named Tam, as two Pauls was too confusing!), Paul McNiff, and all my other housemates, colleagues and friends who were there along the way.

Our lives are intertwined like sprawling vines finding paths towards the sun. While leaves and buds are lost to the winds of history, scars and dents remain, carving out our stories, leaving us forever changed.